*Creating*

*True*

*Prosperity*

# Creating

# True

# Prosperity

### SHAKTI
### GAWAIN

Nataraj Publishing
a division of

NEW WORLD LIBRARY
NOVATO, CALIFORNIA

Nataraj Publishing

*a division of*

New World Library
14 Pamaron Way
Novato, CA 94949

Editorial: Katherine Dieter
Cover design: Alexandra Honig

**Library of Congress Cataloging-in-Publication Data**

Gawain, Shakti, 1948 –
p.     cm.
ISBN 1-57731-170-1 (alk. paper)
1. Wealth – Religious aspects.  2. Success – Religious aspects.
3. Spiritual life.  I. Title
BL65.W42G39  1997                                              97-21304
178–dc21                                                                    CIP

First printing, September 1997
First paperback edition, September 2000
Printed in Canada on acid-free paper
ISBN 10: 1-57731-170-1
ISBN 13: 978-1-57731-170-6
Distributed to the trade by Publishers Group West
10 9

# *Dedication*

To my mother, Elizabeth Gawain, who taught and is still teaching me so much about true prosperity.

# Contents

# Acknowledgments

Katherine Dieter, special thanks for your creative ideas and loving support in helping me shape this project. Kathy Altman, as usual your input was invaluable.

I'd like to acknowledge the team at New World Library, especially Becky Benenate, Jason Gardner, Aaron Kenedi, Marjorie Conte, and Munro Magruder. It's great working with you! Marc Allen, thank you for once again pushing me to write a book.

Thank you Lora O'Connor for handling everything else in my life while I wrote this book.

Hal and Sidra Stone, I appreciate how your guidance has helped me to create greater integration and prosperity in my life.

Jim Burns, thank you for being such a big part of my true prosperity.

# Introduction

About a year ago my friend and fellow publisher Marc
Allen asked me to write a book on prosperity for his
publishing company. At the time I was too busy to
even think about it. Marc persisted, and it eventually
dawned on me that it was a great idea. I had always
intended to write a book someday on the relationship
between money and consciousness.

Normally when I write a book, it is the culmina-
tion of several years of intense focus on a particular
topic. During that time, I study certain ideas and techniques, lead workshops on the subject, refine my
understanding, and of course, work to integrate it into
my own life. By the end, I've really "mined" the topic
for all the value I can get from it. Writing a book is a
way of completing a certain cycle of my own learning
process and passing it on to others.

This book was different. I hadn't been thinking or

talking much about the topic of prosperity in recent years. I knew I had some things to say about it, but hadn't developed or refined those ideas. I had touched on the subject of prosperity in some of my earlier books — *Creative Visualization* and *Living in the Light* — but I knew it was time to update and expand my message.

This project has challenged me to think about and clarify what true prosperity is for me. In the process, I have led seminars on the subject and had some very interesting conversations to learn other people's ideas of true prosperity. In this book I offer you what I have learned. I hope it will be a catalyst for you to discover what true prosperity is for you.

I suggest that before reading further, you take a few moments to close your eyes, and think about what the word prosperity means to you. Don't forget to breathe while you do this! It may help you to begin the process of opening to an experience of greater abundance.

Then, read on....

May this book inspire and assist you in your quest for true prosperity.

With love,

*Shakti Gawain*

# CHAPTER ONE

~

# *What Is Prosperity?*

Most of us think that being prosperous means having plenty of money. So how much is *plenty*? Some people have a fairly clear idea of how much money would make them feel prosperous. "If I earned twice as much as I do now, I would be prosperous," or "If I earned as much as _____ (a specific person they know), I'd feel prosperous," or "Prosperity means being a millionaire," or "Winning the lottery would definitely make me prosperous."

Others define prosperity in a less specific way, something along these lines: "Prosperity would mean having enough money to feel secure about my future," or "Prosperity would be having enough money to do

~

what I want, to have the things I want, and to not feel limited by money concerns. A prosperous person does-n't have to worry about money." In other words, pros-perity is a kind of freedom to be, do, and have what you really want, without much limitation.

Most of us yearn for this kind of liberation from money cares and worries. We think that if only we could somehow earn, inherit, win, beg, borrow, or steal enough money to be prosperous, our financial worries would be over, and the money would probably solve many of our other problems as well!

The question is, how much is enough money to bring us prosperity? Some people have a specific amount in mind they feel would do the trick; others just assume there must be some amount that would work.

Yet the sad fact is that most of us do not experience prosperity no matter how much money we earn or have.

It's easy to see why we don't feel prosperous if we make very little money and have to struggle just to meet our basic needs.

It's also easy to understand why we don't feel pros-perous if we have a moderate income but also have a lot of financial responsibilities: a family to support, a mortgage to pay, and so on.

Yet many people make a considerable amount of money and still do not experience prosperity. Somehow, when our income increases, our level of financial responsibility rises right along with it. The money goes out as fast as it comes in, and we find ourselves under more pressure to manage it all.

I recently read an article about one of the most successful movie stars in Hollywood. The interviewer asked him how it feels to earn several million dollars per movie. He responded, "Well you know, a million dollars doesn't go as far as it used to." Clearly this man was not feeling very prosperous despite what most of us would consider great wealth.

There are often anxieties that accompany having a lot of money: "How do I invest it? How do I manage it? What if I lose it? What if I do something stupid and it all goes down the drain?" We seem to work longer and harder and yet find ourselves missing many important aspects of life — relaxation, intimacy, spiritual connection, fun.

Oddly enough, many wealthy and successful people, especially as they reach middle age or older, find themselves yearning for the kind of simplicity they had earlier in their lives, when they had less money, fewer needs, and more time.

People to whom wealth has come easily, or not necessarily as a result of their own hard work, often experience other pitfalls. Someone who has inherited money, had a lucky break, married a wealthy person, become an overnight success (as with certain actors or musicians), or won the lottery has his or her own set of problems. These may include a lack of self-worth or personal power, inability to manage the money wisely or responsibly (often resulting in losing it), or feeling indebted to or controlled by the source of the money. These people may feel their lives lack direction, meaning, and satisfaction, or feel the tendency to over-indulge themselves to the point of self-destruction.

And there are the reactions of others. Do they genuinely like you or are they just impressed by your wealth? Do they love you for yourself, or do they just want what you can give them? These questions can loom large when you have a lot of money. As you can see, things can disrupt the experience of prosperity at every level of financial wealth.

If you have never been wealthy, it may be difficult to believe or accept that having more money will not automatically make you feel prosperous. Yet you probably know or have met someone who's in this exact predicament — they have more money than you, but they are far from enjoying it. They are unhappy, uptight, and obviously don't feel prosperous. I'm thinking of the brother of one of my best friends who is a successful Madison Avenue executive with a huge salary. Unfortunately he and his family are very unhappy people, always quarreling about their conflicting needs.

I've read many articles about extremely wealthy individuals — multimillionaires or billionaires — who seem intensely driven by the desire to make more and more money. Why? Once you have many millions, how could it matter whether you make another million or two? They don't seem able to enjoy the vast amount of wealth they've created, or able to put it to constructive use. They are obsessed with making more.

At every level of wealth, from the poorest to the richest, there are problems and pitfalls.

When we have very little money, we fear for our very survival. Life is an intense struggle just to take care of basic necessities. We have little opportunity to develop our talents and interests. We feel powerless and perhaps resentful when we see others with more opportunities and luxuries.

As we earn more, we almost inevitably take on more expenses. Life becomes more complex and stressful with so many choices to make. The more successful we become, the harder it can be to sort out our priorities. The more money we have, the more power and responsibility we have to deal with.

When we have wealth, we have to manage it successfully. We become afraid to make mistakes or be taken advantage of. We may be constantly approached by others who want something from us. We have to either face or deny the problem of guilt — "Why should I have so much when others have so little?"

On top of all that, wealth does not guarantee security. There is always the possibility of losing a fortune through bad investment, mismanagement, a lawsuit, a worldwide financial depression, or some other unforeseen calamity. Even a high degree of financial stability cannot bring emotional security. One reason some people continue to pursue money compulsively, even when they have a great deal, is that no amount will ever make them feel secure or powerful.

Having more money, then, does not necessarily bring fewer problems, greater freedom, or security. The truth is, prosperity has less to do with money than most of us believe.

So, what is prosperity?

*Prosperity is the experience of having plenty of what we truly need and want in life, material and otherwise.*

The key point to understand is that prosperity is an internal experience, not an external state, and it is an experience that is not tied to having a certain amount of money. While prosperity is in some ways related to money, it is not caused by money. While no amount of financial wealth can guarantee an experience of prosperity, *it is possible to experience prosperity at almost any level of income*, except when we are unable to meet our basic physical needs.

Problems exist at every level of income. Prosperity can exist at every level, too.

If we think that money has the power to bring us prosperity, we give away our personal power to money. When we give our power away to anyone or anything, we ultimately feel controlled by that person or thing. So, in order not to feel controlled, and therefore limited, by how much money we have or don't have, we must keep our sense of inner power.

We fixate on money because we see it as the *means* to obtaining the things we really want. Often, we forget that it is *only* the means, and it gradually becomes the goal. In the pursuit of money, we lose sight of the end we *truly* desire — what we hope money can buy us. In order to create real prosperity, we need to bring our focus back to discovering what it is we truly want.

If prosperity is the experience of having plenty of what we truly need and want, then in order to experience it, we must do three things:

1. Discover what we truly need and want.
2. Develop the ability to bring those things into our lives.
3. Recognize, appreciate, and enjoy what we have.

Depending on how successful we are with these three steps, we will experience prosperity at any level of financial wealth.

Every one of us is born into this life with the innate power to make our contribution and to create fulfillment for ourselves. However, this power needs to be developed. Most of us have been wounded during the course of our lives in ways that cause us to doubt or deny our own true power. Feeling somewhat helpless to meet our own needs, we repress them. So most of us go through life unconscious of our own real needs and desires.

Deep inside, we feel great yearning, but we don't know exactly what it's for. So we focus on external things — a bigger house, a better job, a relationship — hoping they will bring us satisfaction. Some of them do and some don't, depending on how closely they match what we really want. Ultimately, we don't find lasting satisfaction until we consciously acknowledge our true needs and desires, and learn how to fulfill them.

Start your process of creating greater prosperity in your life by thinking deeply about what you truly want. What is most important to you? What do you need on each of these levels: spiritual, mental, emotional, and physical?

Take time to acknowledge the prosperity you already have. How many of your needs and desires are already being met? Most of us have considerable prosperity in our lives. Often, we are so busy pursuing our unmet desires that we are unable to enjoy all that we already have. Allowing ourselves to really appreciate the prosperity we have created is a big step toward opening to even greater fulfillment.

Remember that creating true prosperity does not necessarily mean *having more*. Many of us are in the predicament of having too much. If we have too many things we don't truly need or want, our lives become overly complicated. This can seriously undermine our experience of prosperity. For many of us, creating true prosperity involves simplifying our lives by clarifying our priorities and letting go of things that we no longer need or that don't bring us real satisfaction. This is especially true for many of us as we reach middle age or older years.

Also keep in mind that we do not exist in a vacuum. Our personal experience of prosperity is inextricably linked with our collective prosperity. Using most of the world's natural resources to provide a small percentage of the world's population with material wealth, and leaving the earth depleted and polluted for future generations is the antithesis of real prosperity. This situation is a reflection of the healing that we need to do individually and collectively.

True prosperity develops as we learn to follow our hearts' true desires and live in balance with ourselves.

~

As we develop this kind of internal integration, we naturally live in greater harmony with others and with the natural world. The greatest personal prosperity can only be experienced in a healthy and prosperous world.

## MONEY AND PROSPERITY

If prosperity isn't *caused* by money, what *is* the relationship between money and prosperity?

It is actually possible, under certain circumstances, to experience great prosperity with no money at all. Imagine living in a beautiful natural environment, building your own home, growing your own food, trading your skills for things you need, engaged in work you love, surrounded by family and community.

Indigenous peoples of the world may have experienced this kind of prosperity, at least intermittently, for many thousands of years. Perhaps some of our more fortunate ancestors may have enjoyed this type of prosperity. Even today, some people live more or less this way, with minimal need for money.

In the modern world, however, most of us choose a lifestyle in which we must deal with money. Therefore our prosperity is related to money in certain ways. For most of us, money plays a part in the process of creating what we want. Our finances are *one aspect* of our prosperity.

I would define true financial prosperity in this way: *Having a relationship with money that supports and enhances our overall experience of prosperity.*

In order to create true financial prosperity, it is important to understand what money is and isn't, and to learn to relate to it in a balanced and effective way.

In the next chapter, we will explore some popular viewpoints on money and prosperity.

# CHAPTER TWO

~

## *Three Viewpoints on Prosperity*

There are three common approaches to money and prosperity:

### MATERIALISTIC VIEWPOINT

From the materialistic viewpoint, we believe that the physical, material world is what is real and important, and that our satisfaction and fulfillment comes from what is around us. Our focus is completely external. Money is the key to getting what we want in the physical realm. In order to find success and happiness, we try to make a lot of money so we can have the things we want and affect the world in the way we desire.

~

This view is probably held by a majority of people in the world today. Certainly most of the people in the Western industrialized world and, perhaps unfortunately, an increasing number of people in developing countries hold this perception. Most of us have either attempted to live this approach, or have rebelled against society's preoccupation with material possessions and financial wealth.

## Transcendent Spiritual Viewpoint

The transcendent spiritual viewpoint of money and prosperity is taken from the transcendent religions of both the East and the West. It is more or less opposite to the materialistic point of view.

The Western transcendent spiritual traditions tell us that the material world is essentially a place of temptation, sin, and suffering, which we must pass through in order to reach a better place — the spiritual realm — after death. The Eastern transcendent traditions teach us that the material world is merely an illusion. The goal is to "wake up" and move beyond the limitation of physical form. Either way, the physical realm is viewed as a prison, a limitation, something to move beyond.

In this approach, truly dedicated spiritual seekers renounce the world and attempt to let go of their attachment to things, in particular money and material possessions. In both the East and West, the most devoted seekers take vows of poverty and give up all but the most simple and basic possessions. They trust that God will provide for them through the mother church or through the people to whom they minister and serve. They attempt, with varying degrees of success, to transcend their own needs and desires for material comfort, security, power, sexuality, and so on.

According to this philosophy, fulfillment comes from the spiritual plane. Prosperity is a richness of spiritual experience. The focus is completely internal. The material world is seen as a seduction away from spirit. We should remove ourselves as much as possible from worldly matters. We should minimize our needs on the physical level, and the emotional level as well. Prosperity comes from simplifying our needs and looking toward our spiritual connection for gratification. Physical poverty can bring spiritual prosperity.

In the materialistic approach, the strategy for creating prosperity is "have more." The more you have, the happier you'll be. In the transcendent spiritual approach, the strategy for prosperity is "need less." The less you need, the happier you'll be.

## NEW AGE VIEWPOINT

Another philosophy is very popular in New Age circles. In this approach, we recognize that the external world is the reflection of our inner world, that the physical realm mirrors our consciousness. "Our life reflects our thoughts" is the popular saying. If we begin to take responsibility for changing our thoughts, our experience of reality will change accordingly.

From this viewpoint, we live in a spiritual universe of infinite abundance. We are limited only by our own thoughts and beliefs about reality. Money is a reflection of our consciousness, and our experience with money is our own creation. Any problems we have with money or prosperity are a reflection of our negative thoughts and our belief in limitation. Unlimited wealth is available if we become willing to acquire it and change our thinking accordingly. We can use techniques such as positive affirmations and various forms of meditation or prayer to help us change our thoughts so that we can open up to the infinite plenty that is our spiritual birthright.

This approach attempts to bridge the internal and the external. The strategy for creating prosperity is, "Change your thinking, and open up to the infinite abundance of spirit, and you can have as much as you want."

## TRUTH AND LIMITATION IN EACH VIEWPOINT

All three of these viewpoints contain elements of truth and may be helpful or appropriate at certain times. Yet I believe each one is too limited to help most of us create true prosperity in our lives.

The materialistic approach can help us develop the skills and abilities we need to survive and succeed in the physical world. It can teach us how to provide for our own physical needs and those of our families and communities. From this viewpoint, we can learn to be comfortable with our own power to make an impact on the world around us. It teaches us to respect and honor the physical plane of existence.

The problem with this philosophy is that it focuses only on the external. It denies the importance of the inner realms and our spiritual, mental, and emotional needs. In this approach, we look for fulfillment only from the physical — and that is never enough.

Ultimately, this leads to a sense of emptiness and dis-appointment because no matter how much we have outside, our inner needs are not necessarily being met.

The transcendent spiritual view offers an escape from the trap of materialism. It acknowledges our absolute need to feel connection with spirit and to feel part of something larger than our individual physical existence. It supports us in exploring and discovering a deeper meaning, purpose, and fulfillment, which can help us release our obsession with the physical realm.

Unfortunately, in swinging to the opposite ex-treme, it creates another trap. It denies the importance of the physical and emotional aspects of our being, and these are important parts of who we are. As spiritual beings, we have chosen to come into human life because there is something very important and mean-ingful for us to experience here. If we deny our physical and emotional needs, we set up a terrible conflict within ourselves. We want and need to be here in the physical realm, exploring, developing, and enjoying it.

I find that most of us who try to follow the tran-scendent philosophy develop tremendous inner con-flict. In pursuing our spiritual development, we are trying to "rise above" our human experience. We try not to want and not to need, yet as human beings, we need and want a great deal! We are pulled between our yearning for spiritual fulfillment and our human needs, or perhaps between the part of us that wants eternal salvation, and the part that wants to enjoy ourselves right now.

We need to trust and honor *all* of our deep needs and feelings. Our desires are the way in which our soul guides us along our path in life. We can only experience true prosperity when we acknowledge and embrace all aspects of who we are — the spiritual, mental, emotional, and physical — rather than placing them in conflict with one another.

The approach of New Age spirituality is on the right track in many ways. Our life *does* reflect our consciousness. The external world is our mirror. As we learn and grow and become more aware, our experience of external reality shifts to reflect those changes. Our relationship with money and our experience of prosperity definitely mirror our internal processes.

The way this philosophy is generally understood and expressed, however, is far too simplistic and limited to address the real issues most of us encounter in our quest to create prosperity.

In fact, in my experience, it can leave people feeling confused and frustrated that they are unable to manifest financial abundance quickly and easily.

We are told that "changing our thoughts" will change our experience of reality and bring us prosperity. However, money and prosperity are not only reflecting our thoughts; they mirror our entire way of living. We are not just minds; we are feelings, souls, and bodies as well. To manifest true prosperity, we must heal and develop *all* levels of our being.

For example, many patterns that block us from prosperity are deeply rooted in our emotional experience. We must become aware of these feelings, and heal the emotional wounds that cause us to act in unconscious and often self-defeating ways. Healing the emotional level is quite a different process than simply thinking positive thoughts.

Also, in order to develop true prosperity, we must learn to tend to the physical level of life, to take care of our bodies, our possessions, our finances, and our environment in responsible and appropriate ways.

Becoming aware of our negative beliefs about money and prosperity, and opening to more positive ideas, is certainly a very important step, but it is rarely enough to bring about financial abundance, let alone true prosperity.

I find the emphasis on "unlimited wealth" tends to put people in conflict with themselves. If they say their prosperity affirmations and money doesn't come, they think, "What's wrong with me? Why can't I do this?"

I don't believe all of us are necessarily meant to have unlimited wealth. On a soul level we all have chosen different purposes and tasks in this life. Some of us may be here to learn to live simply and happily with very little money. Some of us have the challenge of learning to balance all of our personal and family needs on a moderate income. Some of us may be destined to earn and manage large amounts of money and financial power. The essential process is the same: to meet the challenges life brings us in financial and other ways, and to develop the ability to create and experience prosperity.

In the next chapter, I will present another viewpoint, a way of looking at money and prosperity that draws from all these philosophies but goes beyond them. I believe this approach can give us a framework to understand and use our relationship with money as a mirror, guiding us toward true prosperity.

# CHAPTER THREE

~

## *Money Is Our Mirror*

As we have seen, prosperity isn't caused by money, but for most of us, our finances are one important aspect of our prosperity. So if we want to experience prosperity, we have to look at our relationship to money, and understand what it can teach us.

## MONEY REPRESENTS ENERGY

Essentially, money is a symbol for energy. Everything in the universe is made of energy. Physical objects that appear solid really aren't — if we look at them under a powerful microscope, we see they are actually made of vibrating particles. Our bodies, minds, emotions, and spirit all consist of energy.

~

Money is a medium of exchange we have chosen to represent our creative energy. Money itself just consists of pieces of paper or metal. It has little intrinsic value, but we have decided to let it symbolize the energy we exchange with one another. For example, you went out and worked, used your energy in a certain way, and earned money. You used some of that money to buy this book, in exchange for the energy I put into writing it, and the energy the publisher and bookseller used to make it available to you.

Since money symbolizes energy, our financial affairs tend to reflect how our life energy is moving. When our creative energy is flowing freely, often times our finances are as well. If our energy gets blocked, frequently our money does too. For example, a therapist friend of mine has noticed that when she's feeling strong and clear, more clients come to her and she makes more money. When she's feeling spiritually or emotionally blocked, or when she's tired and needs more time to replenish, fewer clients call for appointments.

Actually, everything going on in our life is a reflection of how our energy is moving. Our relationships, our health — all these things reflect the flow of energy moving through us. Money is just another mirror — an incredibly useful one — that reveals what is going on in our consciousness, what is and isn't working.

## MONEY AS A REFLECTION

Everything in our lives reflects our consciousness. Our beliefs, attitudes, expectations, feelings, and emotional patterns are all mirrored in the circumstances and events of our lives. For example, if I am very critical of myself, I'm likely to attract and be attracted to people who mirror that internal process by being critical of me as well. The more I love and support myself emotionally, the more likely I am to attract loving, supportive behavior from others. If I *feel* that life offers me few opportunities, I'm likely to find that to be true in reality. If I have confidence in my abilities, on the other hand, I will probably discover many opportunities to use them.

Money can represent many things to us:

| | | |
|---|---|---|
| security | power | status |
| validation | recognition | worthiness |
| freedom | opportunity | success |
| temptation | evil | greed |
| abundance | happiness | prosperity |

Our financial circumstances will reflect how we feel

about the qualities we consciously or unconsciously associate with money.

If on a deep level we feel unworthy of success or happiness, we may unconsciously prevent ourselves from having much money. Or, if we are deeply insecure, and money represents power and status, we may be compulsively driven to accumulate wealth in the hope that it will bring us the security and validation we yearn for. Yet, at some point, we may lose it all. Seemingly a disaster, this may in fact be our soul's way of setting up an opportunity to become conscious of our deep feelings of inadequacy so we can heal them. Money, or the loss of it, can be a powerful catalyst for our growth and healing.

How does this differ from the popular New Age idea that if we become aware of our negative thoughts and beliefs about money and change them, our financial circumstances will shift to reflect our changed consciousness and we will become wealthy?

First, I am not talking about simply "changing our thoughts." For a real shift to take place in our lives, we must become aware of our core beliefs and our deep emotions — especially the ones that have been unconscious. We must be willing and able to heal ourselves, not just on the mental level, but on the spiritual, emotional, and physical levels as well.

Healing ourselves on the spiritual level involves developing a strong connection with our soul. We heal ourselves on the mental level as we become aware of our core beliefs, release those that limit us, and open to more supportive ideas and greater understanding. Emotional healing takes place as we learn to accept and experience the full range of our feelings. And we heal ourselves on the physical level when we learn to honor and care for our bodies, and for the physical world around us.*

Most of the limiting patterns in our lives are rooted in deep emotional wounds that require a certain amount of time and attention to heal. Even more profound is the spiritual emptiness many of us feel when we experience disconnection from our soul. We can only heal this emptiness by finding a way to reconnect with our spiritual essence.

We are unlikely to achieve real prosperity, financial or otherwise, until we are able to feel comfortable

---

*If you are interested in learning more about the different levels of the healing process, please refer to my book *The Four Levels of Healing: A Guide to Balancing the Physical, Mental, Emotional, and Spiritual Aspects of Life*.

in our physical bodies and know how to operate in the material world, as well.

So there are many aspects to the healing process. This kind of transformation is no simple matter. In fact, it is a gradually unfolding process that lasts our entire lifetime. For most people, it is not enough just to say positive affirmations about prosperity, although that may be one very good step.

As I mentioned earlier, I have a problem with the idea that if we only believe it possible, we can all have unlimited wealth. Perhaps this is true in some ideal, theoretical way. I believe, however, that our souls choose to come into physical life in order to learn and develop in certain ways, and that each of us has a unique journey. Some of us may have chosen to experience extreme physical limitation in this life through an illness or disability, in order to deepen a certain aspect of our strength and wisdom. Similarly, some of us may choose to experience financial limitation at times in our life, or for an entire lifetime, in order to develop certain other aspects of our character.

Often these choices are made on a soul level and we are completely unaware of them. On the level of personality, we might feel quite frustrated and unhappy about the circumstances of our lives until we've done enough healing and consciousness work to begin to understand how our soul's choice is serving us. Remember that no matter what our level of income, we have the opportunity to develop an experience of true prosperity.

Generally, both our relationship with money and our experience of prosperity will develop as a reflection of our healing and growth on all levels.

Here's an example of how money mirrors our personal process: Not long ago, Peter, a business consultant from Germany, told me he had recently made some financial investments that didn't turn out very well. During this period of time, he was not taking very good care of himself physically, emotionally, or spiritually. He was working too hard, driving himself too much. In retrospect, he felt the poor performance of his investments was a direct reflection of the lack of balance in his life. After coming to one of my week-long intensive programs in Hawaii, he committed himself to a deep process of healing on all levels. His financial prosperity reflected this by improving dramatically.

Of course, the mirroring process isn't always this clear-cut for everyone, but this is a good example of how our financial affairs reflect the ways we are learning to take care of our true needs and desires.

Most of us have certain areas of our lives where things generally seem to work fairly smoothly. (Although from time to time we may feel that every aspect of our lives is in chaos!) When something works well, it reflects to us that, for now, we have learned what we need to know in that area.

We may have at least one aspect of our life (and sometimes more) where we feel stuck, where we have problems, or just seem to repeat the same unsatisfying patterns over and over again. Whenever we have difficulties like this, life is reflecting that this is an area where we need increased awareness, healing, and development.

Our lives are incredible mirrors. They show us exactly what steps we need to take in our personal growth at any given moment. We just have to learn to pay attention to these messages.

Most of us have a certain area of our lives where we receive our deepest learning. This is often where we have our most painful problems, as well. If we can discover what we need to learn, and go through the process of healing, our pain will be transformed into wisdom. Often, this proves to be the area where we have the most to contribute and share with others.

In my life, for example, the area of relationships has been the most difficult. This is where I have gone through the most frustration and pain.* However, through this process, I have healed myself of many old patterns, and learned to know and love myself more deeply. The hard work I have done in this area has helped me learn to create deep and meaningful relationships. I believe this learning process has given me a good deal of insight and wisdom, which is part of what I have to share with others.

For some of us, our greatest teacher may be our body. If we have recurring problems with health or weight, the body may be communicating that we need to attend to our healing not only on a physical level, but also on emotional, mental, or spiritual levels. For example, if we tend to push ourselves too hard, our bodies may get sick in order to force us to slow down, relax, and take better care of ourselves. If we learn the lesson our bodies are trying to teach us, and are able to integrate more rest, play, emotional expression, and spiritual renewal into our lives, perhaps our bodies

---

*If you are interested in the details, read my personal story, *Return to the Garden*.

won't have to get sick in order to get our attention.

Some of us may find our greatest struggle, and therefore our deepest learning, in the area of work or career — in trying to find our calling, right livelihood, work that has meaning and purpose for us.

And for some, money is the greatest teacher. If you find yourself constantly struggling with issues about money, regardless of whether you have very little or a great deal, you know that your relationship to money is where you can discover and heal many of your deepest life issues.

## MONEY AS POWER

To understand our relationship with money, it is important to recognize that money gives us power in the world. Having money allows us to do things, to get things, to make things happen. Money gives us a certain ability to make an impact on the world around us. Although it does not *necessarily* enable us to fulfill our spiritual, mental, or emotional needs, it can help us in certain ways to satisfy those needs. For example, money might make it easier to live in an environment that nurtures our spirit, or it might satisfy a yearning to travel. Money can't guarantee us true prosperity, but it *does* represent power to accomplish things on the physical plane.

Our relationship with money reflects how we feel about our power to affect the world. Since money is a mirror of our consciousness, the more comfortable we are with being powerful, the more money we are likely to create in our lives.

Many of us have issues with power, and these are likely to be reflected in our relationship with money. In fact, if you have chronic financial problems, I strongly suggest that you take a deep, honest look at your feelings about power.

If we have issues about power, we generally relate to money by either pursuing or avoiding it. If we crave power, we may pursue money as a way of gaining that power. However, a yearning for power is really how we compensate for a fundamental feeling of powerlessness. We may be driven by the unconscious desire to avoid our deep feelings of fear and helplessness. This is what motivates many people who have great wealth but are obsessed with obtaining more. They can't really enjoy their money or power. No amount of money will ever be enough to take away the fear that is unconsciously held on the emotional level. Money made in this way will never bring an experience of prosperity. Only by consciously acknowledging our fear and vulnerability can we begin the healing process that leads to a true feeling of abundance.

If we are afraid of our power, we may unconsciously keep ourselves from making much money, since to have money is to have power. In fact, struggling with financial need is a very effective way to keep ourselves feeling powerless, and thereby avoid the risks we may associate with power.

I am not implying that everyone in the world who is poor is afraid of power; there are obviously many other factors involved. However, if you live in a culture and an environment of relative financial prosperity and you are experiencing need, ask yourself what part of you might be unconsciously making that choice.

I've worked with many people who have a pattern of struggling to make ends meet financially, and never succeeding beyond just barely making it. Some have a pattern of sabotaging themselves whenever they get close to any kind of worldly success. These patterns generally indicate conflicting feelings about power.

If we have had early life experiences of being physically or emotionally abused by someone with power, or if we have witnessed someone misusing power, we may be deeply imprinted with a fear of power. On one hand, we may be afraid that if we become too *visible* (successful in the world) we will be noticed and abused again. We equate being seen with being unsafe. At the same time, we may fear that if we allow ourselves to become powerful, we will also abuse that power. Unconsciously, we may prefer to remain powerless and struggling rather than take the risk that power may be corruptive or harmful.

A common fear is that our power and success might invoke jealousy or envy from others. Another fear is that worldly power will tempt us or carry us away from things we value in life, such as home and family, simplicity, or spiritual focus.

Obviously, all of these fears have some validity, and cannot be pushed aside or ignored. They must be acknowledged and worked with. A key thing to realize is that we need not go to extremes. We cannot become completely swept up in worldly power, nor can we deny and disown our personal power; we need to find a balance. I will talk about this in greater depth later in the book.

Here is another pattern I've often encountered: If

we weren't cared for in the ways we really needed as a child, that child part of us still lives within us and is still yearning to be taken care of by a parent. The child inside, which we are usually unconscious of, feels that if we grow up and become independent and successful, it will forever lose the opportunity to be cared for. Even though we may consciously wish to succeed, the inner child may sabotage any chance for success and power in the world because it feels it will never receive the nurturing and love it craves. Instead, a pattern of failing develops. This is fueled by the unconscious hope that someday someone will come along and take care of us. This desire is not a bad thing; it's understandable, but we need to bring it into our conscious awareness.

If we become aware of these unconscious patterns, we can begin to heal them. In this case, we need to become aware of the unmet needs of our inner child, and learn how to nurture that child ourselves. This includes asking others for nurturing when appropriate. Once the child is reassured that it can get the love and care it needs, it no longer tries to stop us from owning our power.*

---

*For guidance on healing your inner child, I recommend *Recovery of Your Inner Child* by Lucia Capacchionne, and *Notes From My Inner Child* by Tanha Luvaas.

Again, it's a matter of balance — being vulnerable enough to acknowledge our needs *and* being powerful enough to take responsibility for ourselves. The more comfortable we are with our natural power, as well as our vulnerability, the more comfortable we will be with money and the more likely we will be to draw it into our lives.

Here is an exercise to help you begin to examine your feelings about power and how they might be affecting your relationship with financial prosperity:

Get a pen and paper. Set aside at least twenty or thirty minutes to complete the exercise. Finish the following sentences. Don't labor over them. Respond quickly and spontaneously, without censoring your answers. You can do these exercises several times, over the course of a few weeks or months if you wish.

If I get too powerful I might...

_____

_____

If I get too powerful I might *not*...

_____

_____

My mother thinks power is . . .

_____

_____

My father thinks power is . . .

_____

_____

Powerful people are . . .

_____

_____

Power is dangerous when . . .

_____

_____

A powerful woman is . . .

_____

_____

A powerful man is . . .

_____

_____

The advantage of not being powerful is . . .

_____

_____

If I were wealthy and successful, I would . . .

_____

_____

If I were wealthy and successful, I wouldn't . . .

_____

_____

If you wish, you can do the exercise with a trusted friend and then discuss what comes up for each of you. Or you may want to do some writing about any feelings that arise, or insights you gain.

## MONEY AS A TEACHER

As I've explained, the external reality we experience is a mirror of our internal reality. Whatever is happening "out there" in physical form is a reflection of what's going on inside of us. Since we are usually fairly unconscious of our own core beliefs, assumptions, attitudes about life, deep feelings, and emotional patterns, our external life is a feedback system that can help us become aware of our inner workings.

So every experience in our lives can be a gift — an opportunity to learn something about ourselves through what's being reflected to us, and to use that information to heal and grow.

Therefore, the most positive and empowering way to relate to money is to let it be a teacher for you. Assume that whatever is happening in your financial reality is in some way a reflection of your internal process, something you can learn from, and something that can help you in your self-development.

Regardless of your level of income, if things are flowing along for you fairly smoothly financially, that reflects that your way of living is working well. (Of course, you may be getting signals from *other* aspects of your life, such as your health or your relationships, that are pointing to things within you that need to be healed.)

If you are encountering difficulties financially, this is a reflection telling you that something within you needs to be looked at, some change is needed. The healing needed may be specifically in the area of your relationship to money or power, or it may be something else entirely. For example, it could be a message that you need to nurture yourself more.

This learning process may or may not involve taking external action, but it always involves gaining greater internal awareness. Approached in this way, even an apparent crisis can turn out to be the greatest healing gift of your life.

For example, my friend Liz, a single mother, had been working for many years at a stable, well-paying job at an accounting firm. She had become somewhat bored with the work, but couldn't even consider leaving the job because it provided so much security. Then suddenly she was laid off. She felt angry, betrayed, and frightened about making a living and providing for her children. Seemingly, she was the victim of a terrible misfortune.

When she looked a little deeper to find the gift in the experience, she realized that she had been feeling stuck in a situation that no longer supported her development, but could never have left because of her fears that she would never find anything as good.

She had dreams of other things she would like to do, but had been too afraid to take the risk to try something new. Now, in the face of financial disaster, she was forced to take steps in new directions. Her soul had found a way to keep her moving on her evolutionary journey.

Liz had a good therapist who helped her do some deep emotional healing work with the patterns she had unconsciously inherited from her parents. They had had a very hard time during the Great Depression in the 1930s and were always terrified about survival.

After some trial and error, Liz developed her own business as a consultant, which gave her the opportunity to use the many skills she already had, as well as develop new abilities. Her life is now somewhat less secure but much more exciting and fulfilling.

This experience showed Liz that she had some emotional healing work to do around her fears about survival, and also some work developing new skills. Her financial crisis was really a fabulous gift, which she could probably have received no other way.

I could tell hundreds of similar stories. Many people have written to me or come up to me at workshops and told me how the commitment to looking for the deeper meaning in life's events, and the willingness to learn and grow from everything that happens, has enabled them to find deep healing and wonderful new directions in their lives.

When we follow our intuitive sense of what's true and right for us, and do what we genuinely feel energy for, we always seem to have enough money to be, do, and have the things we truly need and want. I have seen this over and over again in my own life and in the lives of others I know. When we follow the flow of our energy, the universe always seems to support us financially, sometimes in very surprising and unexpected ways.

Here's another thing I've noticed: When we are committed to our personal growth and we feel we need to do something for our learning or healing process, if it is truly right for us, the money will be there to do it. Many people have recounted stories to me of how an unexpected check suddenly arrived in the mail the day before a workshop they wanted to take. My feeling is that if something is right for us, the money will be there to pay for it. If the money isn't there, it may not be right for us, at least not at that time.

It is true that many people become wealthy without being very conscious, because it is possible to create almost anything we focus on strongly enough. This may be the path their soul has chosen for their learning process. Usually, however, the money does not bring a sense of prosperity.

It is also true that some people manifest more money than they can handle responsibly. The problems they encounter may be part of their learning process, a wake-up call for change that may jar them out of their worn-out patterns.

However, once we are committed to a path of consciousness growth, we generally only create as much money in our lives as we can manage responsibly — enough to live on and support our process without distracting us or jeopardizing our journey. As our ability to handle energy and power matures, we tend to generate more money. We usually receive exactly the amount of money we need in order to do the things that are truly right for us. To the degree that we follow our hearts and souls, we will experience this flow of money in our lives as true financial prosperity.

## Tuition

Most of us at some time in our lives have had the experience of making foolish choices about how we spent, lent, or invested some money — trusting the wrong person, being naive, or whatever. Or we've had the experience of acquiring more debt than we can handle, having a business fail, or having to declare bankruptcy. In other words, most of us at one time or another have experienced a loss of money that was significant to us. This kind of experience can be terribly painful, frightening, or embarrassing.

Once, when I had spent money on something that didn't turn out the way I had expected, and I was fuming and grieving about my loss, a friend and financial advisor of mine said, "That's what we call, 'paying our tuition in the school of life!' If we learn what we needed to learn from it, it will not be wasted."

This concept of "tuition" has been enormously comforting to me many times since then, when I have made a less-than-perfect choice of how to spend or manage my money. Now I truly understand that the money is never wasted if it allows me to learn something I need to know.

So if you have recently experienced a financial misjudgment or "mistake," think about it as well-spent tuition in your school of life. Open yourself to receive the greatest learning you can from the experience. Remember that money is a great teacher, and if you are a dedicated student, the tuition you spend will be returned to you many times over.

# Chapter Four

~

## *Understanding Polarities*

One key to creating true prosperity is exploring, developing, and balancing the many energies within us. This chapter and the next two focus on how we can do this.

The physical world is a plane of duality. Life on earth contains an infinite number of polarities. For every truth, there is an equal and opposite truth. Every energy has a corresponding opposite.

Each one of us is a microcosm of the universe; we are born with all the potential energies and archetypes of life within us. One of the greatest challenges in our personal evolution is to develop and integrate into our lives as many of these energies as possible. The more

~

aspects of ourselves we discover and learn to express, the more fullness and wholeness we experience. To do this, we must learn to embrace and balance life's polarities. Let's look at an example of a pair of opposite energies within us.

## POWER AND VULNERABILITY

Every one of us is innately powerful. We are born with potential power; our task is to claim it, develop it, and become comfortable with expressing it in our own unique way. At the same time, we are all innately vulnerable. As human beings, we have needs and feelings that cause us to be deeply sensitive. We all must learn sooner or later to become comfortable with our vulnerability — to acknowledge it and take the responsibility to care for it.

Power and vulnerability are opposite energies. Our power is our ability to affect the world around us. Our vulnerability is our ability to be affected by the world around us. To have a rich, full, and successful experience of life, we need to embrace both these polarities. One of the greatest challenges of the human experience is to learn to live with this paradox: we are both extremely powerful and extremely vulnerable. There are many similar paradoxes that require us to accept all aspects of ourselves. True healing lies in this self-acceptance.

This way of looking at life is quite different than the viewpoint most of us are familiar with. In modern Western culture, we have a very linear, polarized approach to the dualities of life. Instead of seeing them holistically — as equally valuable aspects of a greater whole — we view them as good or bad, right or wrong. From this perspective, we feel we must *choose between* opposites rather than honoring both. We are constantly trying to determine which side of any polarity is correct, good, true, or better. We then support and develop that side while attempting to get rid of its opposite, which we think is bad or wrong.

Not only does this lead to judging ourselves and others, but it ensures we will be in continual conflict within ourselves. Since all of life's energies are innate and essential, we can't get rid of any of them no matter how hard we might try. When we attempt to choose one quality over another, we start an internal war (which, incidentally, is reflected by all the wars we create in the external world).*

---

*Refer to my book *The Path of Transformation* for more information on this.

Let's look at the polarities we discussed — power and vulnerability. In our society, power is generally honored and respected, while vulnerability is judged as weak, embarrassing, and shameful. Because of this cultural bias, most of us attempt to develop our power in one way or another, and eradicate, or at least hide, our vulnerability. This is especially true for men because the traditional bias against vulnerability in men is enormous.

The problem with this stance is that as humans we simply *are* vulnerable. Trying to overcome this fact will not make it go away. At best, we learn to hide it from ourselves and others, which leaves us living in denial. Even sadder, we are attempting to rid ourselves of an essential ingredient to a satisfying life. Our vulnerability is the doorway to our receptivity; without it we cannot receive love, we cannot experience intimacy, we cannot find fulfillment.

People who are overly identified with power and deny their vulnerability may be able to accomplish a great deal. But they will not really be able to receive life's spiritual and emotional rewards, and ultimately may wonder what the point of life is.

Despite our cultural preference for power, many

people consciously or unconsciously choose an opposite path in life. Especially if we've had a damaging experience in our early life with someone who misused power, we may attempt to disown our power. We may identify with vulnerability out of fear that our power might be perceived as a threat or might actually hurt people. Unfortunately, this approach is just as lopsided in an opposite way. Without our power, we cannot accomplish our goals in life, or share our gifts, or properly protect and care for ourselves. A person who is overly identified with vulnerability often becomes a victim of other people or of life's circumstances.

As we discussed in the previous chapter, over-identification with either power or vulnerability often causes some kind of problem with money and prosperity. If we're identified with power, we may pursue money to the exclusion of other important things. If we're identified with vulnerability and disown our power, we may block ourselves from making money or achieving success.

## HONORING ALL ENERGIES

Attempting to choose between the polarities of life — judging certain qualities as "good" or "positive" and others as "bad" or "negative" — causes us to become imbalanced in ways that ultimately become quite painful and frustrating.

Life is always confronting us with the ways that we are lopsided, and nudging — or outright pushing — us in the direction of greater balance. If you are overly identified with power, you may develop an ailment, or lose a relationship or loved one — forcing you to acknowledge and make peace with your vulnerability. If you disown your power, life may force you into a position where you have to stand up for your beliefs, or where you are called on in some way to find your strength.

The key here is this: We must learn to honor all the energies of life. We must understand that for every truth there is an equal and opposite truth. When confronted with a set of polarities — rationality and intuition, for example — we must recognize the value on both sides and somehow grow enough to embrace it all. Once we can make friends with all aspects of ourselves, we have access to our full repertoire of energies. This allows us to approach life's various challenges and experiences much more creatively and appropriately than when we are stuck in rigid roles.

What about the fact that certain energies truly seem negative? For example, if you are a very hard-working person, you might consider the opposite of hard work to be laziness. You might think, "What could be the value in laziness and why would I honor that? Obviously, hard work is good and laziness is bad!" In order to understand this, you have to look underneath the judgmental words you use to describe this polarity. What is the essential quality underneath the judgmental word "lazy"? If you drop the judgment, you might find that quality is "able to relax." Is it possible that as a hardworking person, you could benefit from a greater ability to relax? If so, you must first honor that quality, and acknowledge its value to you.

Remember that we are talking about balance. The idea is not to throw anything out, but to find the appropriate balance of energies that can help you live your life in a more satisfying manner.

This is not a simple concept; embracing the opposites within us requires awareness and understanding. Perhaps the diagrams on the next page can help to make this clearer. The first one is an example of how we may have thought about certain opposites:

## Diagram One: Judgmental View

POSITIVE QUALITIES      NEGATIVE QUALITIES

*Qualities I want*      *Qualities I don't want*

| | |
|---|---|
| Hardworking | Lazy |
| Strong | Weak |
| Caring | Selfish |
| Responsible | Irresponsible |
| Rational | Irrational |
| Organized | Chaotic |

## Diagram Two: Inclusive View

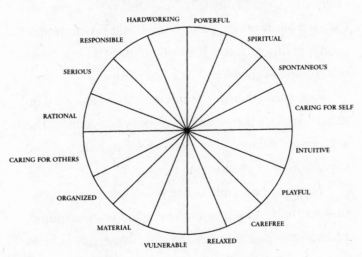

THIS IS ALL PART OF WHO I AM.
*I need and I want all of these qualities.*

~
54

Diagram Two on the opposite page shows the holistic, inclusive perspective — note that the opposites are contained within the whole.

At this point, you may be wondering, "What does this have to do with prosperity?" My response is, "Everything!"

Keep in mind that prosperity is primarily an experience of having what we truly want. When we are out of balance — overly identified with certain energies and disowning their opposites — we experience our life as lopsided, limited, and frustrating. We feel stuck in old roles and patterns. This is not conducive to an experience of prosperity.

The more we learn to accept and express all aspects of who we are, the more freedom, satisfaction, and wholeness we experience, and the more prosperous we feel.

Since our lives mirror our consciousness, the more balanced and integrated we are internally, the better our external world will work. Our relationship with money and our overall experience of prosperity reflect how well we have developed and balanced the many energies within us.

# CHAPTER FIVE

~

## *Exploring Opposites*

Let's look at a few polarities we need to balance in order to experience a high degree of prosperity. Then we will discuss how to go about achieving that balance.

### ACTIVE AND RECEPTIVE

One very important pair of contrasting energies within us is the active and receptive, or dynamic and magnetic aspects. I often refer to these as the fundamental masculine and feminine principles of the universe.

Every one of us, whether man or woman, has both of these aspects within us. We need to develop both of

~

these energies and allow them to work together rather than in conflict with each other.

There are two basic ways to have power or to get what you want in life:

The active mode is to go after it, to make it happen.

The receptive mode is to attract it, magnetize it, allow it to happen.

The active mode requires focus, aggressiveness, confidence, persistence, the ability to do, and the willingness to risk.

The receptive mode requires openness, vulnerability, trust, the ability to be and to wait, and the willingness to have and accept.

In the traditional male and female roles, most men were identified with the active polarity, while most women were more identified with the receptive polarity. A man was responsible for going out into the world to make a living and do what was necessary to support his wife and family. The most important focus of his life was to develop his skills and ability to provide, whether that meant hunting for food or working at a job.

A woman needed to find a husband to protect and provide for her. Her life's focus was to develop her ability to attract the best (most powerful) partner to care for her and their future children.

In the home, things were often reversed — not surprisingly, since a balance always needs to be attained in some way. The wife's responsibility was to take care of her husband and family, to meet their needs for food, clothing, and emotional support. In turn, her husband was expected to *receive* nurturing from his wife in these ways.

This traditional system worked fairly well for a long time, but there were limitations. Everyone was stuck in constrictive gender roles, with little room for expansion or the development of their inner opposite polarities as individuals.

At this point in our evolution, we are challenged to develop both of these polarities within ourselves, and to integrate them into our lives so that we know how and when to use each of them appropriately and effectively.

Most of us are more identified with one or the other of these opposites. We have spent time and energy developing one of these aspects and that's the one we feel most familiar and comfortable with. It's the way we've succeeded thus far, so it's the way we know and trust.

Yet staying overly identified with only one side of this polarity will eventually limit us and cause us increasing pain. If we operate mainly in the active mode, we may accomplish a great deal but are likely to find it a struggle and exhaust ourselves in the process. If we operate mainly in the receptive mode, we may attract many people and opportunities but have difficulty following through with the action that's called for, and therefore feel depressed or inadequate.

So we need to become aware of which polarity we tend to rely on, and learn how to develop its opposite as well. Most truly successful and prosperous people have a balance of both.

Again, our culture is very oriented toward the active masculine mode, so that way is better understood, more honored, and more valued.

I am a good example of a person who has most developed the active polarity. I'm great at making things happen. I can do almost anything I set my mind to. This side of me is very strong; it has helped me accomplish a great deal and become very successful.

However, I tend to take on too much and push myself too hard. When I do this, my life starts to feel like a struggle and I begin to feel burned out and depleted.

When this happens, it is a clear signal to me that I need to let go of the active mode for awhile, and rest in the receptive — relaxing, nurturing myself, and trusting that things will happen as they are meant to. I am reminded at those moments that when I *make* things happen, I may achieve my goals, but when I *allow* things to happen, I create space for the higher power of the universe to bring me much more than I could have imagined. In other words, the universe may actually work better when I don't try to personally control everything!

Learning when to go forward with my active energy and when to relax into my receptive energy is a process I have been working on for many years. My life is far more balanced than it used to be, and as a result, I experience much greater prosperity in all areas of my life. Still, I am constantly challenged to deeper levels of balance and integration. I expect I will be fine-tuning this for the rest of my life.

## GIVING AND RECEIVING

Our abilities to give and to receive are at the core of our capacity to create and experience true prosperity.

We each receive certain gifts when we come into

this life. These gifts take the form of our special talents, interests, and attributes, as well as our universal human characteristics, such as our ability to love and care for one another.

When we do our best to live our truth and express ourselves as authentically as possible, sharing ourselves as we are genuinely moved to, we naturally give our gifts to others and to the world.

In return, we may receive acknowledgment, appreciation, validation, nurturing, love, and in certain circumstances, money or other material rewards. Receiving in these ways allows us to replenish the life force we have "spent," which in turn enables us to continue giving.

So receiving and giving are opposite energies that are inextricably linked together in the natural flow of life, like inhaling and exhaling. If one aspect of that cycle doesn't function, the entire cycle ceases to function and the life force cannot move freely. If you can't inhale, you will soon have nothing to exhale, and before long, your body will be unable to continue living.

This might seem fairly simple and obvious, yet we have enormous confusion in this area. Many of us have difficulty with giving, receiving, or both.

In my observation, the more common problem is the inability to truly receive. There are a number of reasons why receiving is difficult for so many of us. Certainly, one factor is our cultural conditioning. Giving is generally viewed as honorable and praiseworthy. Receiving, or taking, seems perilously close to selfishness, which has a lot of negative connotations for most of us.

Much of this viewpoint comes from our traditional transcendent religious beliefs. If life on earth is a vale of sin and suffering, or an imprisoning illusion, then the more we want or take from it, the more entrapped we become. The less we want, the freer we are to move on to the spiritual realm. In this spiritual ideal, we strive not to need or want. This idea is so pervasive that whether or not we are religiously inclined, our model of goodness is an altruistic person who gives with no thought or desire for themselves.

This ideal is really a fantasy, since anyone who attempts to live only one side of this polarity, denying their natural human needs and desires, will almost inevitably get caught in their own shadow. This is one reason why so many of our spiritual leaders and religious institutions eventually find themselves embroiled in some type of scandal, usually involving sex, money, or power. Our belief is that spiritual people shouldn't be interested in any of these things. But whenever we try to deny any of our natural human needs and desires, they have a way of coming back to haunt us.

Still, we cling strongly to this spiritual model. Almost all of us have heard and been deeply influenced by the adage, "It is more blessed to give than to receive." We might consider changing this to, "It is blessed to give and receive equally for that is the natural, balanced way of life."

We also find it difficult to receive for psychological reasons. The giving position is essentially the power position. When we are giving, we are active. We feel our strength, and we feel virtuous. The receiving end of an interaction is much more vulnerable. In order to receive, we have to acknowledge some need or desire for what is being given. Our discomfort with vulnerability makes receiving very challenging for many of us. It can put us in touch with deep feelings of unworthiness.

Many of us have become very identified with the energy of giving. We are wonderful caretakers, intuitively sensing the needs of others and making sure we provide for their comfort and contentment. This kind of caretaking can be very nurturing for people around us, and at times very satisfying for us. It allows us to feel needed and wanted, as well as strong and generous.

Like most of our other habitual behaviors, however, this is often an unconscious strategy for ensuring our own survival and well-being. If we give enough to others, hopefully they will need and love us so much they will never abandon us. As caretakers we remain in the powerful position of giving to others who appear to have greater needs than we do, and thus avoid dealing with our own fears and needs.

Once again, developing only one side of this polarity eventually leaves us stuck in a limited role. Too much giving can leave us drained and resentful, and encourages others to be overly dependent. If we are strongly identified as caretakers, we must let go of constant giving, and learn how to receive.

One example of difficulty in receiving can be seen in how hard it is for many of us to really receive compliments, acknowledgment, appreciation, or, God forbid, applause! We develop all kinds of creative ways to avoid actually accepting the energy that comes toward us with that kind of attention.

Learning to graciously receive acknowledgment is one small way we can practice learning to receive. If we can learn to receive appreciation, we can more easily receive love, nurturing, success, money, and other forms of energy. I am often in front of large, appreciative audiences, and people frequently express to me their gratitude for how my books or workshops have affected them. At first it was difficult for me to take this in. I have had to learn how to allow myself to receive that appreciation. And now, I must admit, it feels delicious!

Of course, many of us are blocked in the opposite polarity: We have difficulty giving of ourselves to others or to the world. We *hold in* our feelings, *hold back* our expression, and attempt to *hold onto* what we have, including our energy, love, time, money, and possessions. This hoarding posture is rooted in a feeling of scarcity — a fear that there is not enough of what we need, so we'd better hang on to what we've got. This comes from a profound experience of not having important needs met early in life, and oftentimes from not having our natural expression supported or validated. Deep down, we have a feeling of defectiveness or inadequacy — the belief that no one will want what we have to give. This, along with the fear that we will never have enough, can cause us to become overly identified with the need to receive.

We may try to fill our inner emptiness or hunger with addictive behaviors such as overeating, alcohol or drug abuse, obsessive relationships, or the compulsive pursuit of greater and greater wealth. Or, we may become immobilized and depressed.

Just as giving and receiving are both parts of one natural cycle, problems with giving or receiving are just flip sides of the same coin. If we can't give, we can't truly receive and vice versa. These problems are deeply rooted in our earliest life experiences. It takes time and work to heal them. The first and most important step is to look honestly within ourselves and become aware of our feelings and patterns. Another important step is to reach out, and get the help and guidance we may need to do our deep emotional healing work. We'll talk more about that in Chapter Six.

Remember, true receiving takes place when we can acknowledge our needs and desires, when we are comfortable with our vulnerability, and when we feel a basic trust that life will provide for us. True giving takes place when we allow ourselves to receive fully. From that fullness, we naturally desire to share our energy with others.

## DOING AND BEING

*Doing* and *being* are another important pair of opposite energies that are closely related to the ones we've discussed. *Doing* is a state of focused, directed, goal-oriented activity. It enables us to handle the business of life and all the things we need and want to accomplish. Pure *being* is a state where we can fully experience the present moment, without thought of the past or future. It allows us to reach a deeper place, where we can connect with our spiritual nature. *Doing* is primarily the realm of the personality, while *being* takes us into the realm of the soul.

These energies are equally important. Without the ability to do, we would be helpless and frustrated. Without the ability to be, we would feel empty and our lives would seem meaningless. Most of us are more comfortable and developed in one mode or the other. The more we can bring these energies into balance in our lives, the greater our experience of prosperity.

Once again, our culture is very strongly oriented toward the polarity of *doing*. Most of us are taught that we should be accomplishing or producing something almost all of the time. If we are not doing something, we feel we are wasting our time. We admire people who get a lot done, and often feel guilty if we can't measure up to the accomplishments of these supermen and superwomen. Children and adults who are naturally more oriented toward *being* are often considered dreamers, and may be criticized for being lazy and unmotivated.

We seem to have difficulty understanding that spending time *being* is how we replenish and revitalize ourselves. The *being* state allows us to refill ourselves with the life force that we have spent in *doing*. It literally brings us fulfillment. Many brilliant people, including Albert Einstein, have cultivated day-dreaming as a source for their creative ideas.

I frequently encounter people who are so disconnected from *being* energy that they don't really know what it is or how to find it. Most of us experience it spontaneously at certain moments in our lives when we simply feel relaxed, peaceful, and content to be right where we are, with no particular need or desire to do anything else. Often we feel it during quiet moments alone, with a loved one, or in nature. Nature is a wonderful support for *being* because most of creation is primarily in that energy — plants, trees, rocks, rivers, oceans, insects, and animals all radiate *being* energy and can help us find our own. So do infants and young children.

Many spiritual disciplines are focused on helping people move deeply into *being* energy, learning how to "be here now." Any type of meditative practice can help us develop the ability to be. Interestingly enough, many of us connect with *being* energy through some kind of vigorous, rhythmic physical activity such as walking, running, swimming, or dancing.

If all else fails, we have the opportunity to *be* when we sleep. I'm sure one reason why sleep is so important is that it helps us find this balance.

Some individuals are overly identified with *being*, and need to develop more ability to *do*. They have difficulty focusing and following through on their ideas with action. Because they carry the shadow side of this polarity for the whole culture, they often feel like failures, and may be chronically depressed. They need to reach out for support in taking action, one step at a time. Getting their energy in motion, whether it be physically, emotionally, mentally, or spiritually, is the key.

Some people become overdeveloped on the *being* side through long-term devotion to a spiritual practice that emphasizes being in the present moment. They may have difficulty handling the realities of the physical world, including making a living and managing money effectively. They may need to get grounded and learn how to develop "being in action."

## PROSPERITY OF TIME

One of the most interesting aspects of *being* and *doing* energies are their relationship to time.

Time is a very important element of true prosperity. How can we have an experience of satisfaction and fulfillment in our lives if there is never enough time to feel and relish that experience? Yet most people I know, myself certainly included, struggle daily with a reality in which we don't have enough time. In fact, I would say that scarcity of time is one of the greatest problems for modern humans. The richer we become in money and material goods, the more time poverty we experience.

In the past, most people had few options in life. Although life was hard for most, at least it was fairly simple, with few opportunities and choices. Now many of us have a wealth of possibilities, and we try to jam as many as we can into our lives. There are so many things to do, so many options. It's difficult to know what to eliminate, and yet there is just not enough time to do them all.

It seems as if money ought to buy us time. To some extent, it does, but it brings with it more choices and more complications. We may hire someone (or several people) to do things for us — the theory being that we'll free ourselves to do what we prefer, or to do less. Yet many of us discover we spend so much time supervising the people we employ, managing the money, and so on, that we end up feeling *more* time impoverished. If we do liberate some time to pursue other desires, we soon fill it up with new activities!

No wonder many of us begin to envy people who have less money, lead simpler lives, and seem to have a greater abundance of time. In fact, a major social trend is now taking place: Many successful people are choosing to trade financial and material prosperity for simpler lifestyles and greater time prosperity.

This is all integrally related to doing and being. The more identified we are with *doing* energy, the more we find to do. Even if we quit our careers, leave our families, and move to a deserted island, if we don't make an internal shift and develop more ability to *be*, we will soon find ourselves as busy as ever, without enough time for everything we need to do. I know many people who have changed their external circumstances, thinking it would make a difference, and have found it much more difficult than they imagined.

What happens to time when we shift into *being* energy? When we enter the *being* mode, we enter the realm of timelessness. In pure being, there is little sense of time at all — there is just the full, rich experience of the present moment.

We can't live our entire lives from pure *being* energy. However, I have noticed an amazing thing: As we are able to integrate *being* energy into our lives in a healthy balance with *doing* energy, the problem of time begins to dissolve. Because we feel so fed and nourished by our experience of being, we naturally let go of much of our frantic pursuit of external success and even of interesting or exciting experiences. Our own moment-to-moment existence becomes profoundly rich and meaningful. Choices are made from a deep place within. When things need to get done, we feel the energy to do them and they get accomplished fairly effortlessly, or someone else handles them, or it turns out that they didn't need to be done after all. Life becomes a flow, in which we experience our path opening in front of us, exactly as it needs to.

Personally, I am not in this state of balance all of the time, or even most of the time. However, I am balanced more of the time than ever before. It's a gradually unfolding process, an ongoing learning experience for me.

So the next time you wake up in the morning and don't feel like doing anything, if it's possible, honor that feeling and stay with it for awhile. If it's not possible right then, find a time in the near future when you can relax fully into *being* energy. Although it may not be obvious at first, many riches will come from this simple practice. Cultivating a balance of *doing* and *being* energies is the key to experiencing prosperity of time — a very important aspect of true prosperity.

## STRUCTURE AND FLOW

Flow is the natural, spontaneous movement of energy. Structure is the principle that creates order and boundaries. Like every other set of polarities, they are both very important; we need to find an appropriate balance of these energies in order to experience prosperity.

Once again, many of us are more developed and comfortable with one of these principles than the other. Those who are more identified with structure are generally good at managing details and like to plan and organize their lives. Those who identify mainly with flow like to follow their energy as spontaneously as possible, tend to focus on the bigger vision, and pay less attention to details. Structured people often approach things in a more rational, analytical way, while flowing people usually rely more on their intuition and feelings.

It is very interesting to look at these two principles in relationship to how we handle our finances. If we are highly structured, we balance our checkbooks every month, keep a budget, spend money carefully, and think in terms of saving and investing for the future. We track where the money comes from, where it is now, and where it's going.

If we are the flowing type, we generally don't plan or organize our finances very much. We trust that the universe will take care of us, that somehow the money seems to be there when we need it.

Of course, these two types of people often seem to marry each other or go into business together, and drive each other crazy, arguing over the best way to manage money! In reality, they are attracted to each other in part because they each need something the other one has. (We will discuss this more in the next chapter.)

Each one of these approaches to money management has its strengths and its limitations. If we are too heavily identified with one polarity and disown the other, we will eventually suffer consequences. We will be unable to experience the prosperity we yearn for.

If we are overly structured, we may find ourselves working too hard, worrying too much, depriving ourselves of things we really want and would enjoy, and never achieving the sense of security we hope for. We may find our lives lacking pleasure and fun.

On the other hand, if we are too flowing, we may feel ungrounded and unable to confront certain practical aspects of life. We may find ourselves limited in our ability to create success in the world, financially and otherwise. We may even create a financial setback or disaster that signals us that we need to learn how to manage our money.

The bottom line is we need to develop the energies and abilities we don't yet have in order to find balance and experience prosperity. In the next chapter, we'll discover how to do this.

# CHAPTER SIX

~

*Developing Balance and Integration*

How do we develop the many energies within us and integrate them into our lives so that we experience greater balance, wholeness, and prosperity? Much of my own personal growth and my work with others has been focused around this process for many years.

Life is always attempting to move us in the direction of our own evolution and development. This takes place in many different ways. In fact, every experience and event of our lives is part of that process. Most people are relatively unaware of this fact. They are passive participants in their evolutionary journey, or even actively resist it, if life isn't going the way they feel it should. Once we become aware of the fact that life is one big learning experience, it's easier to cooperate with the process. We can actively support and participate in our own healing and growth.

Fortunately, we live in a time when there are many tools, techniques, teachers, guides, and mentors to help us along the way. Of course, some are better than others, and some are right for us at one time in our lives and not at another. It is important to choose carefully who we allow to influence us. Remember that everyone has their human flaws and limitations, even the most seemingly evolved or enlightened.

We can learn much and receive considerable support from others, as long as we don't give our power away to anyone else. It is essential to keep the ultimate authority within ourselves.

I have had many teachers, therapists, and guides at various times on my path, and I have learned, used, and taught many different techniques that have been effective on various levels — spiritual, mental, emotional, and physical.

In the last few years, I have found the work of Drs. Hal and Sidra Stone to be especially helpful to me, and I have incorporated much of their work into my own.

The Stones are psychotherapists who have developed a map of the psyche called the Psychology of Selves, and have created the powerful technique of Voice Dialogue.* Their work is particularly effective in teaching us how to integrate the many diverse energies of life. I am using some of their concepts and terminology in the following section.

## STEPS TOWARD BALANCE

Here are steps I have found can help us to effectively balance our own inner polarities:

*Step One*: The first thing we need to do is recognize that we contain all the different energies of the universe. They live within us as different "selves" or "subpersonalities" within our personality structure. Some of these subpersonalities are already highly developed and form the major part of our conscious personality. These are called our "primary selves." We all have a number of primary selves who generally work together to help us survive and succeed in life. For example, a few of my primary selves are the super-responsible one,

---

*Please see the Resource section for information on their books, tapes, and workshops.

the pusher, the pleaser, the caretaker, the teacher/ healer. We usually develop our primary selves fairly early in life and they generally remain active parts of our personality throughout our lives. They more or less run our lives, making most of our choices and decisions according to what they feel is important.

There are many other energies, or selves, within us that are relatively undeveloped. These are called "disowned selves." Some of these selves may be repressed or held down by the primary selves for fear that they will be harmful or will incur judgment or criticism. For example, my caretaking primary self used to block the energy in me that would put my own needs first, because it feared I would be perceived as selfish.

Some disowned selves may simply be energies that have not yet had an opportunity to develop. For example, I was so serious, responsible, and hardworking all my life that my humorous and fun-loving selves didn't have much opportunity to be expressed. Also, there are certain creative selves in me that I simply haven't yet had time to cultivate.

The disowned selves form the unconscious part of our personality. We may not know about them at all, or we may try to hide them from the world or even from ourselves by denying them. They are what Carl Jung called our "shadow."

However, the disowned selves are important parts of us. Not only can we not get rid of them, we actually *need* the qualities they hold in order to make our lives more balanced, richer, and fuller. So life has a way of putting us into situations where we are forced to confront, acknowledge, and develop our disowned selves.

Our primary selves are usually uncomfortable with our disowned selves and try to keep them from being expressed. The primary selves fear that if these opposite energies come forth, they will take over and control our lives. However, even the primary selves eventually realize that we need some balance. Once the primary selves are reassured that we are searching for balance, and not going to an opposite extreme, they usually become willing to cooperate in the process.

*Step Two*: We need to recognize our main primary selves: What energies have we developed most strongly? What qualities are we most identified with?

If you like, try this exercise: Take a paper and pen and imagine describing yourself as objectively as possible to someone. What words would you use to describe yourself? Write them down on the paper. Concentrate mainly on describing yourself as you *normally* operate in the world. You might imagine how someone who knows you fairly well but not intimately — perhaps a casual friend or co-worker — might describe you. Try not to judge these qualities as good or bad, just describe objectively how you behave a majority of the time. Here are examples of two different people's lists:

| **Karen** | **Ian** |
|---|---|
| Outgoing | Musical |
| Friendly | Quiet |
| Energetic | Artistic |
| Rebellious | Shy |
| Independent | Vegetarian |
| Strong | Humorous |
| Active | Spontaneous |
| Disorganized | Intuitive |
| Talkative | Spiritual |
| Enthusiastic | |
| Athletic | |

Think about some of the polarities I described in the last chapter. Do you identify with any of those qualities? For example, "active," "giving," "doing," "structured." If so, write them down on your list if they aren't already there. Now you probably have a pretty good list of some of your main primary selves.

*Step Three*: Acknowledge and appreciate those primary selves. You may wish to do some writing about this subject. Think about when, why, and how you developed each of your primary selves. Were some of them modeled after one of your parents, or another early role model or influence? Were any of them developed in an effort to be different from a parent or sibling? Are some of your primary selves the disowned selves of the rest of your family? How did it help or serve you to develop the particular primary selves that you did? How have your primary selves helped you to survive or succeed in life? How have they protected you and attempted to take care of you?

Once you've explored these questions and have some sense of how your primary selves have served you, try this exercise:

Close your eyes and imagine one of your primary selves as if it were an actual person. You might see a mental picture of it — how it's dressed, what it's doing

— or you might just get a feeling of it. For example, I imagine my responsible self as a strong woman, slightly stooped from carrying the weight of the world on her shoulders, and feeling really tired. In your mind, imagine thanking that part of you for all that it has done for you. Really let it know that you appreciate the job it has done and is doing for you, and the important role it plays in your life. Let it know that even though you need more balance in your life, and are going to explore some other energies, you never want to lose the qualities this part brings you. You still want it to do its job, but hopefully, that job will become a little easier as you become more balanced.

Now repeat this exercise with each primary self. This may be far too much to do at one time; do it over a period of time, or spontaneously, when you notice that a primary self is active in you.

*Step Four*: Once you begin to become aware of your primary selves, you are no longer one-hundred percent identified with them. You begin to develop a little separation from them. You recognize that they are not *who you are*, they are only *parts* of who you are. Who you are is much bigger and has the ability to contain and express *all* the energies. It's as if you have been looking at the world through a small pair of glasses or binoculars and could only see certain things. You take them off and realize a much bigger world exists.

This experience of separating from our primary selves is the most important step in consciousness growth. The part of us that is able to recognize the primary selves, instead of identifying with them, is called the "aware ego." The job of the aware ego is to keep gaining more consciousness about all our different aspects, without being completely identified with any of them. Once we have begun to develop an aware ego, we have some choice about which parts of us we want to express at any given time. The development of an aware ego is a gradual, life-long process, but every step we take makes a difference.

*Step Five:* Identify some of the disowned selves you need or want to develop. You can start by thinking of the polarities I described in the last chapter. For example, if one of your primary selves is a giver, you may have disowned the part of you that wants to receive. If your primary self is free-flowing, you may have a disowned organizer/planner.

Another way to find out what your disowned selves are is to look at your list of primary selves and think of an opposite for each one. If the words you come up with for the opposites are very negative, see if you can think of the positive essence underneath your negative judgment. Try to think of the value, benefit, or balance this energy might bring you. For example, if one of your primary selves is responsible, and the opposite of that is irresponsible, the positive essence of that quality could be carefree. If you are overly responsible, it could be very healthy for you to find time in your life when you can feel and act carefree.

*Step Six:* Think of some ways you can take small, gradual steps in the direction of developing a disowned self, while still keeping your primary strengths.

If you are very identified with giving, you might start to develop your receiving side, first by just practicing breathing in deeply, letting yourself receive the life force fully. Then, the next time someone pays you a compliment or expresses appreciation, let yourself breathe in deeply and really receive the acknowledgment. After that, you might practice asking for something you need or want — a hug, a listening ear, some help with a project, a small gift. Just keep taking steps to expand your ability to receive, while still enjoying your capacity to give. Take your time with this; it is a gradual process.

If you have disowned some aspects of your creativity, think of steps you can take to get in touch with that part of yourself and begin letting it out. Start with fairly nonthreatening things — reading books on the subject, writing about it in your journal, maybe even doing a small creative project. Then proceed with something a little riskier, like taking lessons or a class, or doing a somewhat larger creative project. Do it for your own enjoyment and try not to worry too much about what others think.

## BALANCING STRUCTURE AND FLOW

Let's look at the polarities I described at the end of the last chapter — structure and flow in the area of finances — as an example of how we can develop the opposite energy of the one we have been identified with.

If you are highly structured and organized, you may need to learn to let go of control a little more — but not completely! Practice listening to your intuition and acting on it. Start with small things at first. You may need to take some financial risks, perhaps buy yourself something you really want that costs a little more than you would usually spend. Eventually you may even need to let go of a job that is no longer right for you and follow your heart in a new direction.

Of course, this kind of shift can bring up tremendous fear that you will lose everything and become a homeless person! That's why it is important to take this process slowly and gradually. There's no need to give up the skills you have that work, such as planning and budgeting. It's just a matter of opening up a bit more to the opposite energy. The idea is to slowly build trust in yourself, and in life. You can follow your own intuitive feelings and move with the flow of life, and you will be taken care of.

If you are a very flowing person, guess what you probably need to do? That's right, balance your checkbook! Not just once, but every single month. You're going to have to start recording all the checks you write faithfully into your check register. You may need to close your old account and open a new one in order to do this. You'll also have to learn to create a budget and live by it.

I have encountered many people who are highly identified with flow, and who are terrified at the idea of confronting and managing the financial details of their lives. They feel that all that stuff is incredibly dry, boring, and limiting and fear it will kill their spirit and destroy life's magic. They also fear that if they actually confront the reality of their situation, they will discover something unpalatable, like the fact that they spend more than they earn.

I have personally taught a number of people how to budget their money. They are often shocked to discover that, rather than limiting them, a budget can be very supportive and freeing. The idea is to face reality and work with it. How much do you actually earn? How much do you really spend? What are your real needs? If you earn less than you spend, how can you simplify your needs for a while or be creative about earning more? A budget should include some of your wishes and desires as well as your needs, and have room for some fun and some extras. A good budget is a guideline for living within your means. It is also a blueprint that can help you create the financial reality you desire.

I recommend you find a good financial advisor, an accountant, or a friend who is good with money, and let them teach you the basics of money management — budgeting, saving, and investing. If you have debts and financial problems, Debtors Anonymous (one of the twelve-step programs) can be a wonderful resource for emotional support, help in coping with your immediate situation, and the opportunity to learn healthier habits. And, it's free! You'll find it in the telephone book in most major cities. If you tend to accumulate debt, seriously consider getting rid of your credit cards. Most people have difficulty managing them well, and for many people they are a real disaster.

Becoming more structured and organized with your finances and your life doesn't mean you have to give up your spontaneity or your trust in the flow of life. It can just help you get more grounded so that you can bring your creative spirit into the world in a more effective way.

## USING THE MIRROR OF LIFE

Often, we are so stuck in our old beliefs and patterns that we aren't able to see the changes we need to make. Even when we feel frustrated about our problems, we may not recognize what we need to learn to change things. That is why we need to use the mirror of life.

As we already discussed in Chapter Three, everything in our lives reflects where we are in the process of developing integration and balance. We can use everything that happens externally as a mirror to help us see the areas within us that need healing and development. Whenever we have a problem, especially a recurring or chronic problem, it is always an arrow pointing directly to some aspect of our psyche where we need more awareness.

If we accept that life is always trying to teach us exactly what we need to learn, we can view everything that happens to us as a gift. Even experiences that are uncomfortable or painful contain within them an important key to our healing, wholeness, and prosperity.

We may have difficulty understanding what the mirror of life is trying to show us, but if we sincerely ask for the learning and the gift in every experience, it will be revealed to us one way or another.

One of the clearest reflections we have to work with is the one provided by our relationships. Everyone we attract into our life is a mirror for us in certain ways. All of our relationships — our families, children, friends, co-workers, neighbors, pets, as well as our romantic partners — reflect certain parts of us. How we feel with someone is usually an indication of how we feel about the parts of us that they mirror.

We all attract certain people into our life who have developed qualities opposite to the ones we are most identified with. In other words, they mirror our disowned selves, and we mirror theirs. These are often the most highly emotionally charged relationships. We either love them, hate them, or both! We feel very attracted to them, and/or very uncomfortable, judgmental, annoyed, or frustrated with them. The stronger the feelings, the more important a mirror they are for us. We have drawn them into our reality to show us something about what we need to develop in ourselves. The fact that we have such strong feelings (one way or another) toward them means that they are showing us a part of ourselves we need to acknowledge, accept, and integrate.

This does not mean we have to be with them or hold onto a harmful or inappropriate relationship. It just means that as long as they are in our lives, or even in our thoughts and feelings, we can use the relationship as a learning experience. It also does not mean we are supposed to become *like them*. They may carry an energy we need more of, but they may be too far to the opposite extreme, or they may express that energy in a distorted way.

Still, we can look for the positive essence in the opposite qualities they carry. For example, if you have been taught never to express any anger, you will probably at some point find yourself in relationship with a person who expresses their anger frequently and vehemently. Life is giving you a strong message that it's time for you to learn to acknowledge your own anger. It is not saying you have to become like this person and go around dumping your anger everywhere. Instead, you need to find the appropriate balance, learning how to assert yourself and stand up for yourself.

If you have strongly developed *being* energy but have difficulty taking action, you may find that someone important in your life is a compulsive doer who can't relax. Naturally, you don't want to go to that extreme, but this person is your teacher, to show you the energy of action that you need to develop. Of course, you are a teacher for them, as well, but it usually doesn't work very well to try to show the other person what they need to learn from you — although we all succumb to this temptation. It works much better to concentrate on what *we* need to learn in the situation.

Once we use the mirror to understand what we need, and actually do the work to develop a disowned self, the whole pattern of the relationship will shift.

If we are strongly identified with power, we will attract vulnerable, needy people. This mirror is reflecting our need to recognize and accept our own vulnerability. If and when we do that, the needy people in our lives will either become more empowered, or will move out of our lives. If we are overly vulnerable and disown power, we will find ourselves in a relationship with someone who uses power one way or another. We will feel overwhelmed, controlled, or victimized by them until we own our power, at which point the relationship will either dissolve or become more equal.

As I mentioned in the last chapter, we often seem to gravitate toward a romantic or business partner who has an opposite approach to financial management. If the difference is not too extreme, this can be a complementary and harmonious balance in which we appreciate and learn from each other's strengths. If we are highly polarized, however, it can be painful and frustrating, leading to a great deal of conflict and stress.

Still, it is a gift — an opportunity to recognize how identified we are with one polarity and a chance to develop the opposite energy we need. Like any relationship issue, it requires that we communicate with one another, and be willing to listen and empathize with each other's feelings and perspective. If we feel stuck in our ability to communicate, it may be an appropriate time to call in a skilled third party — a therapist, marriage counselor, or mediator — to help us through. Personally, I find that most of us need help at certain times to get through the deep issues that are reflected in our intimate relationships.

The topic of relationships is a complex and fascinating subject, which I can only begin to touch on within the scope of this book.* Still, if you grasp the basic idea of how our relationships show us the next steps we need to take in our personal growth, you can begin to use your relationships as powerful guides on your path to true prosperity.

---

* Someday soon I will write a book on this topic! Meanwhile, I recommend the Stones' book *Embracing Each Other*, and several of their audio tapes on relationships.

# CHAPTER SEVEN

~

## Longing and Belonging

If prosperity is an experience of having enough of what we truly need and desire, how do we know what we truly need and desire? We've all had the experience of thinking we need something, or desperately wanting a certain object, experience, or relationship, only to find that: (1) Once we got what we wanted, it didn't make us happy or fulfill us in the way we had hoped, or (2) We didn't get it and life worked out okay anyway.

To make matters more confusing, most of us have been exposed to conflicting philosophies about how we should handle our desires. The materialistic viewpoint says we should try to satisfy all our desires by

~

accumulating wealth, possessions, power, and status. The advertising industry devotes itself to reinforcing and expanding our desires for all sorts of things and experiences. Our Western religions tell us that many of our desires are sinful and lead us down the road to hell. A core premise of the Buddhist philosophy is that desire — or at least *attachment* — is the root of all suffering; the goal is to transcend it. Certain philosophies popular in the New Age movement assure us that we can have everything we desire without limit if we are open to it. No wonder many of us feel uncertain about whether we should pursue or try to let go of our desires.

On an emotional level, we've all experienced not getting our needs met or not having our desires fulfilled in life. As a result, we've all suffered some degree of disappointment, frustration, and pain. If the pain has been great, we may have decided, consciously or unconsciously, to protect ourselves from further disappointment by denying our need and giving up our dreams and desires. Unfortunately, when we shut down in this way, we block the life force from moving through us; we become depressed and numb.

So how do we relate to our needs and desires in a healthy way that can bring us true prosperity?

First of all, let's reflect on the difference between a need and a desire. As I see it, a need is something essential for our survival and basic satisfaction. We have needs on all levels — physical, mental, emotional, and spiritual. Our true desires are our yearnings for the things we feel will enhance and enrich our lives and our development. These are not two separate and sharply defined categories. Rather, our needs and desires exist on a spectrum, something like this:

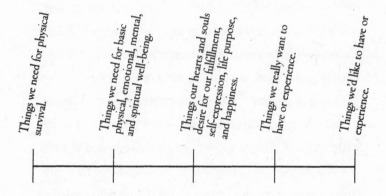

Things we need for physical survival.

Things we need for basic physical, emotional, mental, and spiritual well-being.

Things our hearts and souls desire for our fulfillment, self-expression, life purpose, and happiness.

Things we really want to have or experience.

Things we'd like to have or experience.

Obviously, if our basic survival needs are not met, nothing else is going to matter for long. In general, the further we move along the spectrum, fulfilling each category, the greater our experience of prosperity.

## FALSE CRAVINGS

There is another type of desire, which I call false craving, or addiction. A false craving is something we think we want, but when we get it, it doesn't really satisfy us or enhance our life. We are lured by false cravings when we are not conscious of our true needs and desires, or when we don't know how to fulfill them.

When we pursue a false craving to the point where we become obsessive and out of control, it becomes an addiction. An addiction appears to satisfy some of our needs momentarily, but not for long, because it does not address our *real* needs. In fact, an addiction causes an increasing amount of damage and destruction to our lives and the lives of those around us.

One of the most damaging things about addiction is that it very effectively keeps us from getting in touch with and learning to satisfy our true needs and desires. For that reason, and many others, if we hope to create true prosperity in our lives, we must first acknowledge and begin to heal any addictive patterns we may have. And most of us do have them, to one degree or another.

In this day and age, most of us are aware of a virtual epidemic of drug and alcohol addiction in our society. Also, we are becoming aware of how many of us suffer from serious food addictions such as anorexia and bulimia. Other forms of common addictive behavior include sexual addiction, various forms of obsession about relationships, and workaholism.

Some of these are more subtle than others, and some, like work addiction, are so supported by society they may be difficult to recognize as addictive behavior. Even meditation can become an addiction for some. Anything we do habitually to avoid the pain of not having our real needs met can be an addiction.

There are many forms of addictive behavior related to money. Addiction to gambling is extremely common and destroys many lives and families. Many people have a shopping addiction; we joke a lot about it, but it can be serious if it's used habitually to avoid addressing our real needs and feelings. The compulsive desire to spend money or consume material goods can lead to chronic debt and ruined lives. The obsession to earn more and more money even when one already has considerable wealth is surely an addiction — an attempt to satisfy a chronic craving for security, power, or status. Needless to say, unaddressed and untreated money addictions are guaranteed to sabotage any possibility of enjoying true financial prosperity.

Our addictions are ways we unconsciously try to fill the emptiness we feel inside. This emptiness can only be filled by the things we truly need, such as a deep connection to our spiritual source, a close relationship with the natural world, loving contact with other humans, satisfying work, and a sense of making a contribution. In order to fill those needs, we must allow ourselves to feel them.

An addiction is not something to be ashamed of, although most of us are. We all have them in one form or another. The great thing is when our addictive behavior becomes painful and self-defeating enough, it forces us to begin or deepen our healing process.

We are fortunate enough to live in a time when many resources exist to help and support us in this process. The twelve-step programs such as Alcoholics Anonymous, Al-Anon, Overeaters Anonymous, Gamblers Anonymous, Debtors Anonymous, and so forth seem to be the most effective way for most people to deal with an addictive process. There are also many therapists and support groups that specialize in these issues. If you think you might have an addiction problem, I urge you to reach out for the appropriate help. It could be the most important step toward health, happiness, and true prosperity you ever take!

## DISCOVERING OUR TRUE DESIRES

Once we have begun the healing process with our false cravings and addictions, we can begin to discover our true needs and desires and learn how to go about fulfilling them.

Our true desires come from our heart and soul, and we need to honor and trust them. Life guides us in the direction it wants us to go through our deep longings. Our desires motivate us to move along our path, learning, growing, and developing our unique form of creative expression. Our dreams guide us to the fulfillment of our life purpose.

The poet David Whyte has a wonderful way of playing on the words longing and belonging. We all have a yearning to belong somewhere, to be a part of something greater than our individual aloneness. He says that we can follow our longing to our belonging, that place in life that is uniquely ours as part of the great tapestry of existence.

Here is an exercise to help you get more in touch with your needs and desires:

(1) Find a quiet place where you will be undisturbed for an hour or two, in a comfortable, nurturing

environment. Bring a notebook and pen. Take some time to think deeply about what you truly want in your life, what is most important to you. What do you need on each of these levels: spiritually, mentally, emotionally, and physically?

(2) Write down everything that comes to your mind. Include tangible and intangible things. Remember that some of our needs change at different times in our lives. Include whatever is important to you now.

(3) Then look at each item, and write about why it is important to you. See if you can break everything down to its essential components.

An example:

*I want a beautiful home.*

Why?

*So I can be safe and comfortable, and live in a beautiful environment. I want to express my creative energy through furnishing and decorating it, and create a nest in which to raise my children. Also, I want others to respect the fact that I've earned enough money to buy such a nice house.*

*So, the important elements for me in this desire are safety, comfort, creative self-expression, nurturing my family, recognition from others for my ability to effectively manifest my power in the world.*

As you can see, there are a number of important emotional and creative needs wrapped up in the desire for a seemingly external thing.

Remember that the process of creating prosperity rests on knowing what your needs and desires really are. Recognizing and consciously taking responsibility for your own needs is an essential and powerful step toward creating what you want.

Being conscious of your deeper needs surrounding a desire for a home will powerfully assist you in the process of finding the home that is truly perfect for you. It could be a mansion in the city or a simple cabin in the woods, depending on you and your life journey. If it is right for you, created from an experience of listening deeply to yourself, it won't matter at all what size your house is; you will experience yourself as extremely prosperous in relationship to your home.

The same principles are true for every other area of your life.

Sometimes it is difficult to get started, and the input from friends can be very helpful. Ask five of your friends and/or family members the following questions:

*What do you think I truly want or need that I don't have?*

*Is there any desire in me that you think I'm unaware of?*

Take their responses with a grain of salt. They may be expressing their own needs and desires. However, they may sense things you are not aware of.

## TRUSTING INTUITION

The best way I have found to follow my true desires is to pay attention to my intuitive sense. We all have great wisdom within us, a part of us that knows exactly what we need at every moment. We are born with this intuitive sense, but most of us are quickly taught to distrust and ignore it. We have to relearn something that should come naturally. Fortunately, it's not too difficult; it just takes some practice.

Following your intuition is not some lofty mystical experience. In fact, it is simple and practical — it is learning to trust your gut feelings. It's important to practice with the seemingly small things in life.

A friend recently described this experience to me: She was working on a writing project in her home office when she realized she was feeling quite depressed. A friend called, and when she mentioned how she was feeling, he asked her, "What would lift your spirits?" She instantly felt, "I'd love to get my dog and take a walk outside in this gorgeous weather."

Immediately she felt guilty, knowing how much work she had to do. She forced herself to work for two more hours, but got little accomplished. Finally she took the walk, felt much better, and was inspired to complete the project in time.

This is a simple and beautiful example of how, when we can trust and follow our intuitive feelings about what we need moment by moment, things have a way of working out smoothly. When we don't, we often end up feeling blocked, frustrated, or depressed.

As we discussed in Chapter Six, we have many different voices inside of us, so it does take some practice to learn to distinguish our inner intuitive guidance from the other energies. Our intuitive sense has a particular feeling about it that we can learn to recognize.

Our inner guidance is always within us, but we aren't always able to access or hear it. If we are caught up in our rational mind, we may have difficulty connecting with intuition; we may need to learn to relax and let go of trying to figure things out for a while. If we are emotionally blocked or upset, we may need some emotional nurturing or healing before we can access intuition. Developing a relationship with our intuitive inner guidance is a gradual process, and a very rewarding one.

I have written extensively on this topic in *Developing Intuition* and other books, and I have several tapes with guided meditations on developing intuition and inner guidance. If you'd like to learn more about this subject, I recommend those resources.

In the next chapter, there is a simple exercise to help you practice following your intuition. Listening, trusting, and following your intuition are important steps to true prosperity that bring powerful and oftentimes immediate results.

# Chapter Eight

~

## *Steps to True Prosperity*

True prosperity is not something we create overnight. In fact, it is not a fixed goal, a place where we will finally arrive, or a certain state that we will someday achieve. It is an ongoing process of finding fulfillment that continues to unfold and deepen throughout our lives.

In this chapter, I will outline seven steps on the road to an increasing sense of prosperity. These are not steps that are necessarily taken in any particular order. Rather, they describe different elements of the journey. We each have our own unique path. We may focus on each of these elements at various times and in various ways. At times we may even work on all of them at

~

once. The first four steps are a review and summary of material we have been discussing; the last three are primarily new material.

## STEP ONE: GRATITUDE

Whether or not we feel particularly prosperous at the moment, the truth is that most of us in modern Western society are enormously prosperous, materially and in many other ways. We need only compare our lives with the struggle for survival and subsistence that most humans in history have experienced, and that a majority of people in the world today are still experiencing, to realize how truly fortunate we are. Many of us live better than the kings and queens did a few centuries ago.

Whatever our individual troubles and challenges may be, it's important to pause every now and then to appreciate all that we have, on every level. We need to literally "count our blessings," give thanks for them, allow ourselves to enjoy them, and relish the experience of prosperity we already have.

One simple way to do this is to write a list of every single thing in your life that you feel grateful for and appreciate. Keep the list in a notebook and add to it whenever you think of something else, or whenever something especially good happens. You can even make different pages or different sections in the notebook for each area in your life, such as home, relationships, work, and so on.

When you wake up in the morning or before going to sleep at night, take a minute or two while snuggling luxuriously in your bed to think about what you appreciate in your life. If you are feeling troubled about something, you needn't brush that aside. Acknowledge that feeling as well, and simply let it be there, along with your feelings of gratitude for what *is* working. You may not be able to do this everyday, but remembering to do it as often as possible will enormously expand your experience of prosperity, and create space for more to come.

Make a practice, too, of expressing your appreciation as often as possible to the people in your life who enhance your experience of prosperity in many different ways. Let them know in your words and your deeds how much they mean to you.

## Step Two: Awareness

We all have certain ideas, attitudes, core beliefs, and emotional patterns that limit our experience of prosperity. Deep feelings of unworthiness, a sense of scarcity, fear of failure or success, conflicting feelings and beliefs about money, and many other issues can block our growth and fulfillment.

Also, as we discussed at length, we have each developed certain energies and disowned others, which leaves us out of balance and unequipped to deal effectively with certain aspects of our lives.

Most of these beliefs and patterns are initially unconscious; we are not really aware of them and yet they control our lives. The moment we begin to consciously recognize them, we are on the road to having a real choice about how we live.

The dawning awareness about *what doesn't work* in how we are living is by far the most powerful step in our growth. It is also the most difficult and uncomfortable. As soon as we recognize a problem, we are on the road to healing it. However, that healing takes time. Meanwhile, we may have to watch ourselves repeat the same old self-defeating patterns a few more times.

It's difficult to do this without getting frustrated and self-critical. We need to understand how important this step of awareness is. When you are unconscious, you can repeat a behavior endlessly without gaining much benefit. Once you have some awareness

∼

and can catch yourself repeating the same behavior, you learn an enormous amount. You really feel the pain of it. Then you are able to explore other possible ways of handling the same situation. It's not long before things start to change. You don't have to *make* change. Focus on gaining awareness, and change will follow.

## STEP THREE: HEALING

While we can't force change, we can support and enhance the process of change that we are going through. In Chapter Six I described one powerful way to bring greater balance and wholeness into our lives. There are, of course, many ways to go about supporting our healing and development. Different tools and techniques are appropriate and helpful at different times on our journey, and certain things are helpful to some people and not to others. I believe we know intuitively what is right for us at any given moment and can learn to trust and follow that inner sense.

The work of healing needs to be done on all levels of our existence. I have written about this extensively in *The Four Levels of Healing: A Guide to Balancing the Spiritual, Mental, Emotional, and Physical Aspects of Life*. The book contains many practical suggestions and exercises.

I wish I could offer a simple magic formula for healing your life. There is no quick and easy way, for on a deep level this is truly our life's work. Teachers and healers who promise a quick fix or an easy way are either misguided, or eager to sell their products. (They may offer one piece of the puzzle, however.) I feel we need to surrender to the fact that life is an ongoing adventure in healing and growth, and learn to enjoy the ride!

I also feel that it is very important to get help and support from others as we need it along the way. A good therapist, teacher, healer, support group, wise friend, or mentor can be an invaluable resource for our healing process.

## Step Four: Following Your Truth

We all have within us a deep sense of what we need, and what is right and true for us. To access this we need to pay attention to our feelings and our intuition. We need to learn to listen deeply to ourselves and to trust what we hear. And we need to risk acting on what we feel to be true. Even if we make mistakes, we must do this in order to learn and grow.

~

Here is a simple way to practice paying attention to your inner wisdom:

Find a comfortable, quiet place where you will not be interrupted for a few minutes. It's wonderful to do this outdoors if you can find a place that's really comfortable; a peaceful place indoors is fine, too. Sit or lie down in a comfortable position. Close your eyes and begin to pay attention to your breath. Breathe slowly and deeply. Whenever your mind wanders, gently come back to focusing on your breath and relaxing your body.

Now shift your attention and the focus of your energy down into your heart or belly area. Imagine that a very wise part of you lives in this area of your body, and it has a message for you right now. Ask what the message is, and then relax and pay attention to whatever thought, feeling, or image comes to you. Take whatever comes and be with it for a few moments. Don't worry if you don't fully understand it. Just sit with it a little. Ask your inner guidance if you need to be aware of or be reminded of anything else. Then thank your inner guidance. When you feel complete, open your eyes. If you wish, you can write a little about what you experienced.

Do this simple meditation as often as you can. It's great to do first thing in the morning or last thing at night. With some practice, you will develop your ability to receive and follow your inner guidance.

## STEP FIVE: CREATING A VISION

What would a truly prosperous life look and feel like for you? Where and how would you live? How would you feel about yourself? How would your body feel? What would your relationships be like? What kind of work or creative expression would you have? What other aspects of your lifestyle can you imagine? How would a typical day in your life unfold? How would you feel at the end of your day?

It's important to imagine how you would like things to be. Our imagination is a powerful creative tool. Once we can vividly imagine something, it often opens the door to manifesting it.

Remember that none of us exists in a vacuum. We are powerfully affected by the world around us, and we have an equally powerful effect on the world, whether or not we realize it. We are an integral part of the whole. We can only have a truly prosperous life to the extent that our *world* is prosperous. And our world can only be truly prosperous when we learn to honor and respect the earth we live on, and all the other beings — human and otherwise — who live here as well.

Those of us fortunate enough to live in circumstances where we have the luxury of pursuing personal growth have a responsibility to use what we learn to make the world a healthier, more prosperous place for all.

Since we are all ultimately part of one consciousness, the most effective way to do that is to take responsibility for our own healing. The more conscious and balanced we become, the more we live in integrity and follow our truth, the more healing we bring to the world. We need to ask our inner guidance, too, if there are specific actions we need to take to make our contribution to the world.

Create a vision of prosperity for yourself and the world, in harmony with the earth. You can do this in meditation, or you can write out a description of your vision. Another wonderful thing is to make an actual picture of it by drawing or painting it, or make a collage by collecting photos, cards, pictures and words cut out of magazines, elements from nature — anything that has meaning to you — and gluing them onto a large piece of paper or cardboard. Hang it on your wall, and it becomes your treasure map — every time you look at it, you will give energy to your vision.

## STEP SIX: SETTING GOALS

Once you have a sense of your overall vision for a truly prosperous life, you can set some specific goals. There are times in life when it is helpful to set goals, and other times when it is best to let go of goals for a while and just see where life takes you. If you check in with yourself and it doesn't feel right, skip the goals process for now. If it feels exciting, fun, or helpful, go ahead and give it a try.

You might start by creating a special notebook for your goals. Think of the different aspects of your life that are important and make a list of them. For example:

Personal Growth

Health/Appearance

Relationships

Work/Career

Finances

Home/Possessions

Recreation/Travel

Creative Expression/Special Interests

Making a Difference/Service

Write one of these categories at the top of each page.

Then think about your relatively long-term goals. Where would you like to be in five to ten years, in each of these areas? Write one or two long-term goals for each aspect of your life on the appropriate page. If you like, you can write your goals in the form of affirmations, in the present tense, as if they were already true.*

Go through the process once again, this time creating one or two one-year goals in each category. Try to be realistic with your one-year goals; pie in the sky will only set you up for disappointment.

Now go back through each category, and write down one to three reasonable steps you can take toward each goal. Choose a few of these steps to take within the next month or so.

Here are some examples of long-term goals, shorter term goals, and action steps:

*Work/Career*
Long-term goal: To become a family therapist.

---

* For an explanation of affirmations, please refer to my book *Creative Visualization*.

One-year goal: To go back to college and complete my
   master's degree.
Action steps:
   1. Call local colleges and have them send me information and applications.
   2. Read through materials and decide which
schools interest me.
   3. Complete and send in application.

*Creative Expression*
Long-term goal: To learn to play the piano.
One-year goal: To take piano lessons.
Action steps:
   1. Ask musician friends about possible teachers.
   2. Call piano store about renting a piano.

Once you have created your goals, put them away
for a while. Look at them occasionally and update
them as needed. Be sure to appreciate yourself for the
steps you have taken, and the progress you have made.

Goals can help us gain clarity, inspiration, and
focus. However, they can also work against us if we
hold onto them too tightly, or try too hard to make
them happen. Try to let go of your attachment to
having them happen in a certain time or way. Don't

worry about how to make them happen; let the higher creative power handle the details.

Hold your goals lightly, and allow them to change and evolve as you do. You may find that certain things are going as you hoped, while others aren't. You may even find your whole life is going in a different direction than you expected. Remember that our souls have a purpose in this life that we may not fully understand yet, and everything that happens to us is part of our soul's journey.

Learn from everything that comes your way. Continue to follow your intuitive sense. If a certain goal is right for you, it will unfold naturally from this process. Let your inner guidance show you the way.

## STEP SEVEN: SHARING YOUR GIFTS

As you follow these steps, you will find yourself naturally expressing and developing the special talents and abilities that you brought into this life. When you follow your heart, and are committed to your healing and growth, you simply can't help becoming more and more of who you are meant to be!

Often we have difficulty recognizing and appreciating our own talents, because they come so naturally to us that they don't seem like a big deal. The things we find ourselves gravitating toward, the things we can't help doing, are important indications of what we are here to do. The things we feel passionate about are clues to our life purpose.

Ask yourself, "What do I love to do? What do I just naturally find myself doing?" For example, I just can't help talking about consciousness growth. I'm fascinated by the process, and passionate about sharing it with people. As things have unfolded, I've ended up teaching and writing about personal growth for a living. I did not plan this, nor could I have predicted it. It's what evolved as I followed my interests and desires.

Unless we are blocked in our ability to succeed or receive, life always rewards us appropriately for what we give. Through answering what calls us, we develop our right livelihood. Essentially, the universe pays us to be ourselves, as fully as possible!

The opportunity to share our gifts and thereby make a difference in the world is one of the most profoundly fulfilling experiences we can have in life, and an essential ingredient in creating true prosperity. As we live our lives with integrity and passion, our experience of prosperity just keeps expanding.

~

# CHAPTER NINE

~

# A Conversation with Shakti

*As Shakti and I worked on this book we had several inter-esting conversations in which I asked her questions about various topics in the book. We thought it would be valuable to our readers to share some of these questions and answers.*

— Katherine Dieter, Editor

Q: *Identifying my needs sounds so simple, but I'm forty years old and I still don't feel clear about them. There are so many things: more time alone, socializing, money, and free time — things that seem to conflict with each other. Where do I start?*

A: It can be difficult to know what we need and to sort out our main priorities. Mostly, you just have to start paying attention.

What do you really *yearn* for? Think about what people experience when they go through a disaster and lose everything. They quickly reassess their lives.

~

What would be most important to you in this situation? What do you truly need and want for your wellbeing?

Yes, a lot of different voices inside say conflicting things because, as I've said, life is filled with polarities. We do need time alone, and we do need connection with others. But you might find, for example, that general socializing is less important than having deep, regular contact with a few people.

You might discover that you can eliminate some of the less fulfilling ways you relate to others, pursue the ones that bring you greater satisfaction, and have a little more time to yourself.

I realize it is not easy. But it is the process of becoming more and more aware. We have to go through life with the question, "What is truly important to me?" And keep refining the answer. Our needs and desires change. As we pursue certain things that feel important and develop certain aspects of ourselves as a result, our priorities may shift.

For example, my work has been a huge part of my satisfaction and fulfillment in life for a long time. That's beginning to shift slightly. I've fulfilled a lot of my needs and desires in that area. I'm feeling the need for more personal time, and the desire to explore other areas of my creativity. This is causing me to develop new ways of working, as well.

Q: *Why do I seem to know what my family and friends need, but not what I need?*

A: If you have been identified with being a caretaker or a pleaser, you may find it much easier to know other people's needs than to know your own. You have to learn how to take some of the attention off others and focus on yourself.

It takes practice, like anything else we try to master. Most of us have been conditioned not to recognize our deep needs. We haven't learned how to be sensitive to ourselves in that way. With some support and practice, you can learn to do it.

Q: *What if I have a million issues — health, money, relationship? Where do I begin?*

A: When you have a million issues, it usually means that some basic underlying issues are showing themselves in many different ways. Look for the underlying *core issues* you're grappling with, on whatever level —

emotional, spiritual, physical, mental — and work on those. If you start looking deeper to find out what's really going on under the surface, almost any issue you take, whether it is money or relationships or health, boils down to the same life lessons you need for your growth.

Q: *You say an important part of prosperity depends on balancing polarities — in life and in ourselves. Does that mean that the happier and more prosperous I get, the more drastic downturns I can expect?*

A: No, quite the opposite. If you are identified with one side of a polarity, and you live your life primarily from that side, then sooner or later, life may force you over to the other side so that you begin to explore and accept the other polarity.

If you have done the conscious work to become aware of and accept both sides of any given polarity, then you're already "containing" both of those opposites. It's a very stable position. Once you develop both aspects, or at least have awareness and acceptance of both, it stabilizes you. You're much less likely to experience a negative extreme.

Q: *I have this fear of becoming too happy because then I'll have to be equally sad. Will something upsetting have to happen to me?*

A: If you only want happiness in life, and you will accept nothing but happiness, you're totally identified with one polarity and you're denying the other one, probably out of fear. Sure enough, life is probably going to come along and force you to experience sadness.

But if you have an acceptance of both polarities, if you understand that human life consists of moments of happiness and moments of sadness, you ride through the times of sadness, knowing there is another side to it. Life's fullness and satisfaction isn't stripped away just because you're going through a difficult moment.

Q: *I have less money than I did five years ago, but I feel more prosperous. How is this so? Is it because I'm less afraid now, or because I'm in denial? Is it progress or denial?*

A: I would guess that it's progress. It fits right in with the fact that prosperity depends less on our financial situation than on the extent to which our needs are being met in life.

~

It's likely that you have evolved to a place where you're more in touch with yourself in certain ways, and consequently, more of your needs are being met — perhaps not all of them, but more of them. If you're more aligned and connected with yourself, it may be irrelevant that your money situation has shifted slightly.

Q: *And if it has shifted more than slightly in a negative direction? Wake up and smell the interest payments, right?*

A: Then you probably need to ask yourself what your financial situation might be reflecting to you. You may need to take another step of change or healing.

Q: *Would you please talk about resistance? For example, we may know what's good for us, but we still can't do it. Anyone who has ever been on a diet or suffered addiction has run into this.*

A: When we resist something, it's important to acknowledge the resistance, honor it, and find out what it's about. We tend to put ourselves down for feeling resistant. When we have resistance, there is a reason for it. Rather than trying to push past it, or make it go away, we have to stop right where we are and acknowledge what is true for us in that moment.

For example: "Some part of me doesn't want to do this right now and in fact is actually *stopping* me from doing it. So what is that, and why does it feel that way?"

Honor what is stopping you. Check in with it directly. When you do that, you usually find a valid reason. Once we acknowledge and pay attention to the resistance, and honor it as part of the whole, things can begin to shift.

You may need to look at how identified you are with rules, with the authoritarian voice within you. Authoritarian energy always provokes rebellious energy, both inside our psyche, and in interactions we have with others.

*Resisting is a reaction to insisting.* Who inside you is doing the insisting? If you find one part of you pushing very hard to do things a certain way, it may bring up rebellious or resistant energy.

Q: *Is this related to addictions?*

A: People with serious addiction issues, almost invariably, have strongly authoritarian inner voices, usually reflecting the values of their parents, family, or religion. Rebellious energy develops in reaction to authoritarianism and becomes aligned with an addictive process.

The inner dialogue goes something like this:

Authoritarian voice: "You should work hard and be very serious and responsible all the time! You should eat only wholesome nutritious food! You should go to church every Sunday! You should be a perfect parent to your children! You should think only positive thoughts!" Etc., etc.

Rebellious voice: "Oh yeah? I think I'll go out and have a drink!" (Or eat some ice cream, or whatever.)

The addictive behavior temporarily numbs and silences the authoritarian voice. However, the next morning it's back, stronger than ever:

Authoritarian voice: "Well, I must say you really blew it last night! Now you'll have to work twice as hard to be a decent person!"

The interaction of these energies plays itself out over and over again, until the person gains some awareness and is able to make more conscious choices.

Q: *"Not enough" is my middle name. The only way I know how to handle this persistent feeling is to affirm otherwise. Is there anything else I can do?*

A: Affirmations are always helpful, but I think getting in there and working with the part of you that feels that way would be even more beneficial.

Most likely, the child in you is feeling inadequate or defective. We all have a wounded child, and we have to consciously acknowledge it and work with it. How can you help her, a child who feels so bad about herself? How can you bring in some of your strengths to support that part of you, instead of running over her or pretending she doesn't exist? You may need to get some help from a therapist or support group to learn how to do this. It's a deep process that takes time, but it's certainly related to your ability to experience prosperity.

Q: *Is there any such thing as* not *being in a pattern?*

A: Yes, we have moments of real consciousness, which means that for brief periods, we may be free of our unconscious patterns. Then we fall back into them. We re-emerge for a moment or a day of clarity. Even if we haven't consciously focused on personal growth, just aging and maturing usually gives us greater insight and awareness about our patterns. We're able to let go of things that don't work for us and do things that work better. If we focus on and commit to personal growth, our consciousness increases as we go through life. It can get better and better as we get older. And it does.

Q: *It's hard for me to imagine anyone working on being more vulnerable. To me, being vulnerable means being hurt. Can one really heal enough to willingly be vulnerable? What does this involve?*

A: Yes, you can be willing to be vulnerable. We need to be — because we *are*. Vulnerability is part of human experience. We *are* able to be hurt. The paradox is that you can only feel deeply loved and accepted for who you are if you can show your vulnerability and feel that it's accepted.

Having the strength and support within to take care of yourself makes it safe to acknowledge vulnerability. This doesn't mean you won't ever get hurt, because we do get hurt in life; but if you have enough strength and commitment to yourself, you won't allow yourself to be abused. If you know a situation is frightening or hurtful, you will do what you need to do to take care of yourself as best you can. Then, in a certain way, you limit your vulnerability. You don't just throw yourself out there in the world in a way that lets everybody walk all over you. It is vulnerability with appropriate protection and strength supporting it.

Q: *I attended one of your speaking engagements on prosperity recently and noticed that when you said that not everyone's journey includes making a lot of money, a wave of disappointment passed through the room. (I know I felt disappointed; I had already picked out a new yacht.) How do you respond to this reaction?*

A: I believe that, on a deep level, it is a choice. Some God out there hasn't decided, "Okay, you're going to be rich and you're going to be poor and condemned to poverty for life. Now, make the best of it."

I think our soul makes a choice about what kind of learning process it wants in this life, or what we need for our development as human beings. I feel we are all challenged to find true prosperity within the particular circumstances we've created in our lives.

Q: *I refuse to believe that my soul's journey may include being broke throughout my life. Does the fact that I use the word "refuse," with its highly charged feeling, mean I have a disowned energy or aspect within me?*

A: It very well might because when an emotional charge is present, disowned energy is usually lurking. You may be disowning the part of you that could be happy with very little — the ascetic within you.

Also a part of you may feel, "If I never have a lot of money, I'll never get my needs met."

That's like being condemned to unhappiness for the rest of your life. What if you *could* be happy living a simple life with only the money you need to do the things you really want, and feel fulfilled by that life? Would it have to include huge amounts of money?

Q: *I've gotten used to charging things in a pinch and thinking the money will always appear. Are you familiar with the voice that says, "I will not live within my means?" (It's like Scarlet O'Hara in* Gone with the Wind: *"I'll never go hungry again!") How does one tame this Scarlet O'Hara with a Mastercard?*

A: We're talking about rebellious energy again. Credit cards are very, very tricky. And I would have to advise people to be extremely careful. If you have any tendency toward self-sabotage, rebellion, or extravagance, it is probably best not to use one. Even extremely judicious, super-responsible people are surprised by how quickly it all adds up and have trouble paying them off. Credit cards cater to the parts of us that don't want to acknowledge boundaries.

Q: *I always expected myself to make a very good living, better than my parents, and it's not happening. Any ideas?*

A: Chances are you are identified with an aspect of yourself that sounds like this: "If you're a successful person, you should make *this* amount of money; you should make more than your parents did because your standard of living is supposed to progress."

You may have denied or disowned a part of you that sounds more like this: "I don't really care about having a lot of money. I don't even care about having a fabulously successful career. If I could live in a lovely place, do something I love, have loving people around me, and enjoy my days, I'd be just fine."

Of course, another possibility is that you are unconsciously blocking your own ability to make more money, out of fear of power or success, or out of rebellion.

Q: *How can I create a budget when my income is extremely erratic?*

A: My income is erratic and always has been. I do my best to estimate what I think will happen. I'll project a few months ahead or a year ahead, month by month, based on how many workshops I'm doing, what my book royalties might look like, and so forth. I try to project fairly conservatively so that I won't have any nasty surprises. With practice, you can learn to make fairly educated guesses.

Then, you just have to keep revising it. It is very important to look at how much you're spending. One key I find in budgeting is that once you have real clarity about your spending needs, somehow you manage to create the income to cover those needs. This has been my experience, and I've seen it happen for others time and time again.

Q: *Doesn't budgeting limit one's idea of prosperity? Wouldn't the time be better spent in visualizing more income?*

A: No, because when you budget, you create a blueprint of what you need. That allows the universe to come in and fill it. I find that it works best to take conscious charge of the process, find out what you need, and *then* visualize the income you want. Then just keep expanding your vision a little at a time.

Most people think a budget tells them what they *can't* spend. A good budget is balanced; it makes room for some things you want, as well as things you need. You may not be able to spend as much as you wish right now, but with some patience, your financial prosperity will increase.

Q: *I'm afraid the more balanced I get, the more boring and uninteresting I'll become. Any suggestions?*

A: It has to do with the image you have of being balanced. Being balanced does not necessarily mean that you're constrained to walk the middle ground. It actually means working with a full range of energies. It means consciously moving between extremes, which gives you tremendous freedom and plenty of options.

With awareness, you begin to have some choice about which parts of you come out when. They all have their place and there is room for all of them. When you take responsibility for, and get comfortable with, all aspects of yourself, you've got a tremendous range of energies to work with, and are even able to go from one extreme to the other. You can embrace and express your wild woman, your Aphrodite, your hedonist, your ascetic, your child, and many others.

From this place, you can express and experience the entire range of your being, according to whatever feels appropriate in the moment. The point is you get to choose, rather than just have it happen to you.

Q: *The main thing that interrupts my experience of prosperity is fear. Is it true that our fear will haunt us until we do the thing we're most afraid of? I have thought about jumping out of a plane to get rid of my intense fear of heights.*

A: You have to acknowledge your fear and work with it. I don't believe that it's a good idea to push past your fear and force yourself to do things that you're terrified of doing. I think it's better addressed by looking at the fear, being with the fear, honoring and supporting it, and then discussing what small step you could take in the direction of healing that fear.

I think of the fear in me as a frightened child. What would be the best way to deal with a frightened child? If you have a child who is afraid of heights, would you push her out of an airplane?

No, that isn't the best way to handle this situation. A more appropriate way would be to sit down and talk with this child gently and lovingly, and let the child express everything that's going on for her.

Perhaps a strong, pushy voice is saying, "Come on, this is what you should do."

And that kind of power energy nearly guarantees that the opposite polarity — the vulnerable energy of the child — will come up: "But I'm scared, I don't want to do that."

Try saying to the child, "Let's see now, if we *wanted* to do this, what could we do to make it a little less scary for you?"

Through this process, you begin to align your power and strength *in support* of the frightened, vulnerable aspect of yourself. You don't push it, or deny it, saying, "Oh, you're so stupid for being scared," or "Get out there and do it."

Many of us have used our strength to deny, suppress, and punish our vulnerability. We have to learn to use our strength to support our vulnerability. A child who feels she's being listened to, cared for, supported, and encouraged becomes less and less frightened.

We can take smaller steps and our fear won't block us in life. If we don't take steps bigger than our fear can handle, we will progress.

Q: *Do you think one can do this kind of process alone or is it necessary to have a facilitator or therapist?*

A: I think having a good facilitator or therapist can be very important. Most of us treat ourselves the way our parents or other significant figures in our early life treated us. In many ways, therapy is reparenting. It's being with somebody who shows you how to do it differently. Once you have a certain amount of experience with a facilitator — an experience of someone else being there for you — it becomes easier to do for yourself.

Q: *"Balancing polarities" makes me think I have to force myself to do things I don't want to do. Is this a misconception?*

A: Yes, it is. You don't have to *force* yourself to do things that you don't want to do. You might, on occasion, have to give yourself a little push in a direction that is difficult or challenging for you, but it shouldn't feel like forcing. If it does feel that way, don't do it. It should feel more like exploring, like something you want to do but are unsure about. It is stretching, not forcing. Life has a way of moving us along in whatever direction we need to go.

Q: *Do you feel any more secure than you did before you became a successful author and teacher?*

A: Security hasn't been a big issue for me, perhaps because I was raised by a strong, adventurous mother.

But yes, I do have more confidence in myself now,

because I've proven to myself that I can be successful in the world. I have a track record of contributing, doing it well, being acknowledged by the world, and making a good living from it.

I have experienced more insecurity in the emotional realm of relationships. That's where it has been more difficult for me. And yes, I now feel more secure there, too.

Q: *Is there a part of you, a disowned self perhaps, that thinks that becoming conscious is a bunch of hooey, that it's not something humans have control over but rather something that happens to them?*

A: Let me put it this way: I have a very healthy skeptical voice. It is not disowned at all. In fact it may be one of my primary selves. When I started to get involved in personal growth, I had to test everything out on a very practical level to see if it worked. After years of doing this work, I feel certain that making a commitment to our consciousness growth does enable us to make huge changes in our lives. And of course I've seen how my own life has evolved as a result of following these principles. I still have to test out new ideas and prove them to myself, though.

Q: *Do you have any comments on the commercialization of spirituality?*

A: That question seems to come from the traditional transcendent view that money and spirit are opposites. That view holds that money represents something nonspiritual, and you don't want to have spirituality contaminated by money. If you understand that money is a symbol for life energy, there's nothing wrong with paying someone an appropriate amount for useful information and guidance.

If teachers are offering false promises to people in order to get money, they are simply out of integrity. It doesn't matter whether you're offering a used car or ten steps to enlightenment; if you give misleading information, you are out of integrity.

Q: *Why should I have so much wealth when others have so little? What makes me more "deserving"?*

A: First of all, you may be assuming that there is a finite amount. You think if your piece of the pie expands, other people will have a smaller piece. But money is a reflection of energy and there is plenty of life energy to go around. It is possible for each of us to learn to live more in the flow, allowing more energy to move through us and our lives.

On the other hand, there are a finite amount of physical resources in the world, so it is true that we need to be aware of how we use those resources. We have created an unbalanced situation, where too few of us are consuming too many of the world's resources.

We can have as much energy flowing through our life in the form of money as the universe deems fit, but I do think that we have to be conscious of how we are living on the earth and not consume its finite resources.

If you find yourself with more money than you feel you "deserve," you can use this as a way to make your contribution to life. Use that energy, use those resources, to do what you feel moved to do. It will serve as a model to others that it is okay to have that energy and power. I talk a lot about this in both *Creative Visualization* and *Living in the Light*. It comes down to the fact that if you follow your heart, soul, and true desire, money comes in a way that isn't harmful to you or anyone else.

Q: *Recent books on prosperity talk about following your bliss and finding work that is fun and exciting, but nothing is fun and exciting on an ongoing basis, is it?*

A: Yes, some things are fun and exciting on an ongoing basis. Nothing I know of is fun and exciting every single minute; everything has its difficult moments, its challenges, its problems, and its frustrations. When you're doing what you love, or what's right for you, it can be very enlivening and satisfying.

"Following your bliss" is a lovely phrase, but it does make it sound like you're supposed to be in bliss all the time. And I don't think it's like that. I don't know anyone who experiences their life that way. No matter how much they love what they do, it isn't bliss all the time.

I do believe that when we follow what really excites us, what we really have energy for in life, we experience a high degree of involvement, fascination, fulfillment, and yes, even fun!

Q: *I was raised with the idea that if something is fun, it isn't work, and that one should be paid according to difficulty.*

A: I don't think anything you work at over time is

ever *just* fun. But it is possible to get paid well to do things that you deeply enjoy. I do. As much as my work is fun, it can be a problem, at times, too. But most of what I do comes straight from my heart and soul, and I really do enjoy it.

Q: *Why does Buddhism tell us that desire is the root of all suffering and freedom lies in letting go of our attachments, while you say to trust and follow our desires?*

A: I've heard many different translations and interpretations of this teaching. I'm not sure what Buddha had in mind, but I'd like to think that perhaps he was referring to the false cravings we experience when we lose connection with our hearts and souls. However, I've observed that the way many people try to apply this teaching leads to denial of one's human needs and feelings, and a constant inner battle with oneself. Rather than struggling to *free* ourselves from our human experience, it seems to me that it works much better to recognize that as spiritual beings we've *chosen* this human experience. My path is to embrace it, honor it, explore it, learn from it, and enjoy it as fully as possible.

# CHAPTER TEN

~

## Stories of Prosperity

Here are a number of true stories that explore various aspects of prosperity. Some of these stories may give you food for thought, and others may inspire you.

> This is the story of my dear friend Manuela Terra-Luna, a wise and radiantly beautiful woman who is living a life of simple and profound prosperity.
>
> Manuela has essentially led her life as a gypsy. She has kept herself unencumbered by major financial responsibilities, so she is free to follow her heart and change her life completely whenever she feels so moved. In all the years I have known her, I have

~

*observed that she always has* exactly *the amount of money she needs to take her next step — no more, no less.*

*To me, she is an example of the freedom and prosperity that can come when we do the inner work to know ourselves deeply, and when we keep our needs simple so that we can follow our intuitive guidance.*

## Simple Prosperity

Manuela was born in Italy during World War II, with bombs exploding all around. Her mother died when she was three and she grew up in an orphanage run by nuns. Her childhood was unbelievably regimented, and lacked both warmth and affection. As soon as she was old enough to leave, she got a job and an apartment and began to explore freedom for the first time.

In her early twenties she came to the U.S., fell in love with and married an American man, and had a daughter. For the next twenty years she worked at various jobs and developed her many creative talents. Among other things, she wrote and performed songs in Italian, created and sold beautiful collages, and studied filmmaking, working for a time as a film casting director and an assistant to Francis Ford Coppola. She also devoted herself to a path of personal healing and growth, working with many different teachers.

After going through a divorce, she came to live and work with me as my personal assistant. I found her to be one of the most conscious, intuitive, and delightful people I had ever encountered, and she soon became one of my best friends.

After a few years of working with me and focusing on deep emotional healing from her divorce, Manuela suddenly felt a strong pull to return to Italy. This surprised her, as she had never intended to live there again. Still, the feeling was so strong, she set off with almost no money and even less of an idea of what she was meant to do there.

Although she had been to many personal growth workshops, she had never had any interest in leading them. Now she felt prompted to offer workshops in Italy. As things unfolded, she became very successful traveling all over Italy teaching and training people in the ideas and techniques she had studied. She attracted many devoted students who trained with her for several years so that they could carry on the work. Needless to say, her presence had a powerful impact on many people's lives.

After five years, despite her success and the ongoing demand for her work, she intuitively felt that she was finishing this process and it was time to come back to the U.S. Once again she had no idea where she would live or what she would do.

In Italy, she met and married Luigi, a wonderful man twenty-six years younger than her. Once again she was challenged to follow her heart, despite the unorthodox age difference. Together they came to the island of Kaua'i, where I have a home. Manuela soon realized she no longer wanted to teach. Instead, she was drawn to gardening and working with the earth.

She and Luigi now have jobs as caretakers on a beautiful property. They live in a cottage on a spectacular estate that sits on a cliff above a gorgeous beach. At the moment, they are both thrilled and fulfilled to be expressing their creativity through landscaping and gardening. They are deeply committed to each other; it is a true soulmate relationship. While their income is very modest, their financial needs are minimal. They live in paradise, they are following their hearts, their lives are simple and deeply fulfilling. And I can hardly wait to see what Manuela does next! ∼

*My friend Frank is a marvelous example of the prosperity that can result when we risk letting go of what no longer works, and follow our dreams.*

## Taking the Risk
### Contributed by Frank Kramer

Once upon a time, I had a brilliant career with a large, well-respected financial institution. My job was prestigious and highly lucrative, and promised life-long financial security. Yet, I was unhappy and deeply disturbed about the quality of my life. It occurred to me that I didn't really have a life, I had a career.

The burnout from my job was getting so severe — including bouts of depression — that I began to search for ways to move on. As a skilled manager of people, I was highly educated in planning, strategy, and goal-setting. Yet, all of my efforts to find a new career seemed futile. I couldn't seem to find a direction. So, I gave up and did exactly what I would have advised anyone against: I quit without having another job.

Recently divorced, with substantial obligations for alimony and child support, I can't claim that I acted out of wisdom and courage. It was more like desperation. I had a vague idea of what I wanted to do, but it seemed like an unattainable dream.

The few years that followed turned out to be more interesting and inspiring than I could have ever imagined. Although I was living month to month, in financial uncertainty, I was so grateful to feel alive and in touch with myself, I didn't mind not having money. I began writing poetry, discovering nature, and reading books about new ideas I'd never encountered before — like *Creative Visualization*.

I am amazed at the way things happened for me. I couldn't have mapped out a more brilliant strategy than what actually happened, purely by "accident."

I have always been fascinated by how companies get started, raise money, and go public. As I began to learn about this, doors opened I never knew existed. My accountant mentioned that he was leaving his firm to start a company with some other associates and asked if I could help them raise money. So I did. I learned as I went along, made many mistakes, but never regretted it for one minute. After a few years of "paying my dues," some of the deals I put together began to pay off. Now I have the luxury of working when I feel like it and doing what I enjoy.

I attribute my ability to play as one of the most

important qualifications for what I do. Growing up in Louisiana, I had a knack for telling Cajun jokes. One day I created a routine and entered a Cajun joke telling contest. I carried that act on to a few night clubs, and now enjoy performing at various places around town. I also write children's poetry, which has been published in various magazines and in my own book. Here's a sample:

### Retirement

I am frequently told
that when I get old
I'm entitled
to draw some retirement.
I am certain by then
at a hundred and ten
I will have
pretty simple requirements:
some breathable air,
a story to share and
laughter to tickle my mind,
some food and some water
and stuff I can barter
for a clock,
that reverses the time!

One of the advantages of having been broke, depressed, and feeling like a failure, is that it is familiar territory; the fear of failure is so much worse than "failure" itself. Having attained a lifestyle that I only dreamed about, I have come to realize that there is no destination, only life's continuing journey — fraught with detours, setbacks, and surprising twists and turns. The journey is so enchanting for me, that these risks are well worth it. ∼

*Here is a true story from my own life that shows the mysterious ways in which the universe often works to meet our needs and bring us prosperity.*

## Hurricane Iniki to the Rescue

I have a beautiful piece of property with a large house on the island of Kaua'i. Kai Mana more or less fell into my hands a number of years ago at a very reasonable price with almost no down payment. I bought it with the idea of holding retreats but soon encountered zoning problems, so it became a bed and breakfast where people can come for personal retreats and vacations.

I do not feel that I "own" this land. To me, the idea that a human being with a lifespan of a few decades can own a piece of the Earth, which has been around for millions of years, is remarkably arrogant and basically laughable. I feel this land has been given to me to care for and steward. It is a powerful, healing environment, and I feel it is meant to be shared with others in appropriate ways.

There is a large mortgage on the property that has, at times, been a heavy financial burden for me. Yet I feel this is something I was meant to do, and somehow I have always managed.

The house's kitchen and bathrooms were in bad shape when I bought it, and they have steadily deteriorated. A few years ago it became clear that a major remodeling was urgently needed. I refinanced the property and borrowed $60,000 — enough to do adequate but not top-quality remodeling. I knew it would take me a few months to get organized and get the plans drawn, so I put the money into a short-term investment at a good interest rate with a friend of mine. He was a stable, trustworthy businessman. I had invested with him before, and it had worked out well.

When the time came for him to return the money, he confessed that he was going bankrupt and had lost it all. I had no recourse; I had simply lost $60,000, which I now owed to the bank. I had no money for the remodeling.

I was shocked and completely at a loss as to what to do. I prayed to understand why this had happened and what I was meant to learn from it. I also asked for guidance about the needed repairs. In essence I said to the universe, "Okay, you gave me this place, now you show me how I'm meant to take care of it!" Meanwhile, I canceled the remodeling plans and watched my kitchen cabinets decaying in the Kaua'i humidity.

Three months later Kaua'i was hit by Hurricane Iniki. No lives were lost, but the island suffered massive physical destruction. Everyone was shaken to the core. As always with such events, people were forced to re-examine their lives and priorities. It caused great hardship for many, yet much healing, change, and transformation resulted.

The roof of our house was lifted off and blown over the cliff. Humans and animals were all unharmed, but there was enormous damage. Like everyone on Kaua'i, we were without electricity and telephones for several months.

Eventually, however, we received a large insurance settlement. In repairing the house, we were able to rebuild it much more beautifully than before. If I had not lost the money and had proceeded with my former plans, the remodeling would have been of a lower quality, and much of it would have been damaged by the hurricane anyway. So the time, energy, and money put into it would have been wasted.

I certainly don't believe we had a hurricane on Kaua'i just so I could get my kitchen remodeled! To me, however, this is a remarkable example of how events often work together synchronistically. It also demonstrates how apparent disasters — my personal financial loss and the devastating hurricane — can turn out to be powerful transformational events that can lead to greater prosperity on many levels. This is one of the many, many events in my life where a higher power seems to be at work. And as a result, I now live in a lovelier home, which people from all over the world now enjoy as a healing retreat. ~

*This is a true story anonymously contributed. As you can imagine, since winning the lottery, "Suzanne" has lost some privacy and gained some previously unheard-of friends and relatives.*

## Lottery Winner

My childhood friend and I grew up in very similar circumstances. Our mothers waitressed together for ten years. We considered ourselves "middle-class." Our parents owned homes in the suburbs, but doing that meant our mothers and fathers all worked full time or more. We were the first generation to attend college, and those of us who did also worked during our college years. I'll call my friend Suzanne.

Suzanne married soon after high school and had a child. She had been waitressing since her teens and continued to do so. When her child was about nine years old, the improbable happened — she won nearly $30 million in a state lottery. Her sister, a statistics aficionado, figured that the chances of this happening were about the same as the chance of one person being hit by lightning twice!

Her husband seemed to benefit tremendously. Immediately his health and outlook improved. He seemed to really enjoy the transition and began to feel truly prosperous.

Suzanne, however, found the transition more difficult. From a very young age, much of her self-respect and even her identity revolved around being able to do much with very little — the ability to save for her child's college education for instance, or buy a house on a limited income by pinching pennies and doing without luxuries. How was she supposed to feel in this new role? Who was she now? What would she do with all the coupons she'd collected?

Her primary selves — from my perspective — were a combination of Hard Worker, Pusher, and Survivor. These "selves" had no idea how to deal with such a windfall. She felt guilty, undeserving, and at a loss in the midst of this new financial abundance. Three years later, she is finding her way through these new feelings and questions. She's not complaining about her situation, but her current definition of prosperity has less to do with money and more to do with her relationship to self, family, and the world around her.

We all imagine we would like to have these challenges. But it just goes to show, as someone once said, "Wherever you go, there you are." ~

## Sometimes Less Is More
Contributed by Katherine Dieter

Tom was born in a small town in northern Minnesota. He grew up in a blue-collar, Scandinavian family in the 1950s. When he finished high school and wanted to attend college, he was able to borrow a small amount of money from his father, and for this he remains grateful. As he puts it, however, the money didn't come with strings attached, it came with cables — meaning he had little choice about what he would study. After completing college (and promptly paying his dad back) he was determined to do things differently with his children when they came along. And they did come along, four of them.

In a very short time, about ten years, he created a tremendously successful accounting firm; he even owned a private jet, which had been a childhood dream. While he represented some of the most successful recording artists of the sixties and seventies, he began to feel vaguely dissatisfied. He had achieved everything imaginable materially — a massive estate, several cars, his jet — but his personal life was suffering.

He did not have the energy for his family he had hoped for. His children were growing up quickly and he felt he was sacrificing his relationship with them in order to acquire more "stuff." He felt a distance between him and them remarkably similar to the distance between himself and his own father. The only difference was that Tom had a choice. His father had to spend most of his time away from his family to support them.

Upon realizing this, Tom made some drastic changes, the first of which was selling the jet. Had it been important enough, he would have kept it. But he discovered its importance had dwindled, along with the importance of all his other possessions. He readjusted his priorities. He scaled back his involvement in the business and created more time with his wife and children. He began to focus on the aspects of the business that were most enjoyable to him. He let go of the clients he didn't enjoy working with. He sold the country estate. He began to develop the relationship with his children that he truly desired.

Not surprisingly, the business continued to flourish. He had delegated carefully, and it thrived over the following ten years. When it came time for his son to enter college, he did so with the sincere support of his father, who knew him well. When it came time to pay tuition, he offered it without cables attached. The ability to do this was more important to Tom than the money itself. ~

## A Life-Changing Dream
Contributed by Marc Allen

I came of age in the turbulent and wonderful 1960s. I tried all through my twenties to live without paying any attention at all to earning a living, or even to the entire "material plane of existence." It taught me at least a couple of things: (1) The universe somehow provides for us, as if by magic, if we do what we love to do, but (2) If we don't take care of ourselves we will end up living off other people. We live in a capitalist system and need a certain amount of money to function in the world. This fact cannot be ignored. We're all forced to deal with it one way or another.

When I was thirty, Shakti and I began a small business publishing our books and tapes. Our first few years we spent much more money then we made.

Part of the problem, when I thought about it, was that I had many negative beliefs about money in general and business success in particular. I feared that if I succeeded, I would somehow lose my soul. I would no longer be a spiritual person. I would become jaded, greedy, consumed by materialism. I would veer off-course, and forget my purpose in life. Then one night I had a dream:

I was climbing a mountain with rocky outcroppings; it was a difficult climb. Then I found a graded road that ascended the mountain more gradually but made the walking much easier. I saw a cave that went deep into the mountain, but the entrance was blocked by an elaborate wrought-iron gate. I fiddled with the tangled iron in the center of the gate, and pulled out a sword with a wrought-iron handle. Then the gate opened! I went into a dark cave. It was scary, but I had my sword to protect me.

After a journey through a dark tunnel, I entered a huge vaulted, cathedral-like room. A large banquet table was spread in front of me, filled with all kinds of things: gold, piles of money, jewelry, musical instruments, flowers, little houses, little cars, books, tapes, candelabras, food — piles and piles of stuff. And a wordless voice said to me, *This is the material plane. There is nothing to reject in it. It is here for you to enjoy — and to master. Have fun with it!*

I awoke with a deep sense of peace and joy. That dream was somehow worth years of therapy. There is nothing to reject, there is beauty and wonder in all of life. Making money doesn't automatically turn you into a monster. It gives you a powerful tool for good in the world, the power to make a difference, the power to make your dreams come true.

After that dream, my business prospered. I was no longer working against myself, consciously or unconsciously. ~

# Full Circle
## Contributed by Becky Benenate

I lost my father at an early age. My mother, who had never completed high school, was not able to cope with raising four children alone. She knew she had to go back to school in order to have any future and made the difficult decision to send three of her four children to foster homes. I was one of the three. From the age of eleven to seventeen I lived in five different homes — not the greatest esteem builder. I was emotionally lost with no religious or spiritual foundation. I would often daydream about the happy times when my family was together — Mom, Dad, my two sisters, and my brother.

I became obsessed with the idea of someday getting married, creating my own family, and giving my family everything I lost as a child — security, love, trust, commitment. I knew *my* family would be perfect and no one could take it away from me!

I married at the age of twenty-three. My daughter was born three years later. When my daughter was just over a year old, my husband and I bought the American Dream — a four-bedroom, two-bath home, complete with all the amenities. I had everything I thought

I ever wanted. Then why was I so miserable? If I had everything I wanted, why didn't I feel happy and prosperous? These questions led me on a path of self-discovery and personal improvement.

I started reading everything I could get my hands on regarding personal growth. My two favorite books were, and continue to be, *Living in the Light* by Shakti Gawain and *The Nature of Personal Reality: A Seth Book* by Jane Roberts. These books, and many others, helped me a great deal. I started going to workshops and seminars. I started meditating and practicing yoga. I began to develop an incredible inner push to continue on a path of personal growth. I wanted to know who I really was and what I wanted in life. I needed to find my life's purpose.

I left my sweet family, not fully understanding why. I gave up my home and the savings we had acquired as a family. I left with nothing. I moved nearly 400 miles away to understand who I was and what I was about. I had no family, or friends. I simply moved because it felt right at the time. I had no connections in the community and the country was going through a recession at the time, making it difficult to find work.

Eighteen months passed, and I still hadn't found a

job. In the meantime, I lived off of credit cards. I paid for my rent, my food, my car payment, my insurance, everything you can imagine for day-to-day living, with credit cards. Suddenly I was $45,000 in debt.

I abandoned my quest for personal growth, feeling I had convinced myself of something that just wasn't true. Maybe my ex-husband was right, maybe I *had* totally lost my mind. Just as I thought I was going to die of depression, I was offered a job. To this day I don't know how I managed to get through the interview without appearing desperate. Perhaps they just felt sorry for me. Finally, things started to turn around.

Slowly, I began to re-establish my relationship with my spiritual and personal growth. I started to trust my intuitive feelings again. Books were my lifesaver. I began to create balance in my life, and was finally able to take care of my basic needs.

A few years after I started my job, I began to feel it was time to stop working just to survive and time to create a position in the field I felt most passionate about. I wanted to be involved with inspiring books, the same kind of books that kept me going during my worst times. I wanted to give back to all the authors and publishers whose work had helped me.

When I look back I'm amazed at all of the lessons I learned during those difficult times. I eventually *did* create the job I wanted in publishing, and I am blessed with the opportunity to help authors like Shakti create their next works — to give back to those who gave me so much. I am blessed because I found and live my life purpose!

And finally, I have the family I always wanted. Last year my siblings and I were brought together for the first time in twenty-three years. Developing relationships with them is slow, but it's happening. I now have a better relationship with my ex-husband than I did when we were married — we are very good friends, with a deeper understanding and respect for each other. I have a wonderful relationship with my daughter who, now at age twelve, is coming to live with me. I continue to grow both personally and spiritually. And, financially, I've paid off all of my debts and own my own home.

The path to true prosperity isn't always a smooth one. I created all of my so-called troubles. But I'm grateful for the lessons I learned along the way because I love the person I became through the process. If we are willing to learn the lessons life is teaching us, keep

love in our hearts, and truly live our life's purpose —
prosperity is ours! ~

*To me, my mother is a shining example of someone who has created a life of simple prosperity in her later years. At seventy-six, she lives on a modest, limited income, yet is enjoying her life fully.*

*She lives in a lovely rented cottage on the island of Maui. Each morning after a breakfast of tropical fruit, she putters around in her beautiful garden and then goes for a swim in the ocean.*

*Here is her own description of her life:*

## A Wealth of Time
### Contributed by Beth Gawain

One of the many wonderful aspects of growing older is that we begin to have time. It is a marvelous luxury, after one retires, to wake in the morning able to decide, on the spur of the moment, "What do I want to do today?"

When I stopped working in my career as a city planner, one of the first things I did was to get a bird book and persuade my niece (an educated naturalist) to take me bird watching. I had always been interested in birds, but she had to show me the simplest things, such as how to find the birds among the leaves or grasses. At first I used my family heirloom mother-of-pearl opera glasses! Now after years of travel and bird-watching, I have a long list of birds I've seen on four continents.

I took up yoga practice a number of years ago, and still do that regularly. I'd always wanted to learn to paint with watercolors. So now I do that. Most recently I learned to make pottery, and have made all my dishes, vases, flowerpots, even a birdbath for my yard. It's a glorious feeling to have time to pursue these new interests without cramming them into an already over-busy schedule.

I remember that, a couple of years into my retirement, my daughter became a devotee of the Day-Timer organizer book. She gave me one for Christmas, and enthusiastically began showing me how to use it. I was overwhelmed with *resistance*! The last thing in the world I wanted to do was fill my life with schedules. This was hard for her to grasp. I had always been a busy working mother who went to night meetings, wrote reports and speeches on weekends, published the newsletter for Parents without Partners, and was vice president of the co-op.

Now when I meet people who knew me in those

years, they ask, "What are you doing nowadays?" My favorite answer is, "As little as possible!" Another good answer is in Italian: "Dolce far niente." (Sweet to do nothing.)

That brings me to the most important point. Having time to do things I never had time for is a great freedom, but the greatest freedom of all is to have the choice to do *nothing*.

Doing nothing in our busy culture is not easy. It requires a big shift in values, and a significant change of habits. And then it requires practice. The impulse to start doing something, anything, is very powerful at first.

A great way to begin, I think, is in nature. I can easily spend an hour just sitting on my lanai watching the palm leaves swaying in the breeze, or watching ants scurry along. I love to watch raindrops falling on banana leaves, beading like quicksilver. And of course watching ocean waves wash in and out, my whole soul gets into the primordial rhythm. Or I can just float around in the warm ocean, not even swimming. I like to feel that I can "do nothing, not even meditate."

I believe it is important for those of us who are elders to be an example in the world of taking great pleasure in quiet time. Our culture has so little silence, so much noise and busy-ness. Our standard greeting is, "How are you doing?" or "What are you up to?" Even our classic greeting when being formally introduced is, "How do you do?" We ask, "How are you feeling?" only if someone has been sick — and then we hope they won't go on and on about it. At least now we sometimes say, "How are you?" — but we usually just answer, "I'm fine."

Does anyone ever ask, "What have you been wondering about?" or, "What have you been contemplating?"

Our culture places so much value on eventfulness and excitement. Can we learn to value silence, peace, serenity? Can we take time for that?

Elder years can bring a wealth of time for going places and doing things we couldn't do in years of career and family responsibilities. It also allows us to take quiet time. Now we have a wealth of time for contemplation and silence. We have plenty of time for being. ~

*I hope you have enjoyed these stories. If you have an inspiring or thought-provoking true story related to some aspect of true prosperity from your own life or someone you know, I invite you to send it to me. It could be anywhere from one paragraph to two pages long — please, no longer. Please type it neatly, and include your name, address, and telephone number. I look forward to reading them! And who knows? I might create a book of prosperity stories. Please send to:*

Shakti Gawain
Prosperity Stories
P.O. Box 377
Mill Valley, CA 94941
E-mail: staff@shaktigawain.com

# RESOURCES

~

Allen, Marc. *Visionary Business: An Entrepreneur's Guide to Success*. New World Library, 1995.

Capacchione, Lucia. *Recovery of Your Inner Child*. Simon & Schuster, 1991.

Gawain, Shakti. *Awakening: A Daily Guide to Conscious Living*. Nataraj Publishing, 1993.

Gawain, Shakti. *Creative Visualization*. New World Library, 1978.

Gawain, Shakti. *Developing Intuition*. New World Library, 2000.

Gawain, Shakti. *Four Levels of Healing: A Guide to Balancing the Spiritual, Mental, Emotional, and Physical Aspects of Life*. Nataraj Publishing, 1997.

Gawain, Shakti (with Laurel King). *Living in the Light: A Guide to Personal and Planetary Transformation*. Nataraj Publishing, 1993.

Gawain, Shakti. *The Path of Transformation: How Healing Ourselves Can Change the World*. Nataraj Publishing, 1993.

Gawain, Shakti. *Return to the Garden: A Journey of Discovery*. Nataraj Publishing, 1993.

Orman, Suze. *The Nine Steps to Financial Freedom*. Crown, 1997.

Stone, Hal and Sidra. *Embracing Our Selves: The Voice Dialogue Manual*. Nataraj Publishing, 1993.

Stone, Hal and Sidra. *Embracing Each Other: Relationship as Teacher, Healer, and Guide*. Nataraj Publishing, 1993.

Stone, Hal and Sidra. *Embracing Your Inner Critic: Turning Self-Criticism into a Creative Asset*. HarperSanFrancisco, 1993.

Stone, Hal and Sidra. *The Shadow King: The Invisible Force that Holds Women Back*. Nataraj Publishing, 1997.

Whyte, David. *The House of Belonging*. Many Rivers Press, 1997.

~

## *Audiotapes*

**Gawain, Shakti**
*Creating True Prosperity*. New World Library, 1997.
*Creative Visualization: Book on Tape*. New World Library, 1995.
*Creative Visualization Meditations*. New World Library, 1996.
*Developing Intuition*. Nataraj Publishing/New World Library, 2000.
*The Four Levels of Healing: A Guide to Balancing the Spiritual, Mental,
    Emotional, and Physical Aspects of Life*. Nataraj Publishing, 1997.
*Living in the Light: Book on Tape*. Abridged version. Nataraj
    Publishing, 1993.
*Meditations*. New World Library, 1997.
*The Path of Transformation: Book on Tape*. Abridged version.
    Nataraj Publishing, 1993.

**Stone, Hal and Sidra**
*The Child Within*. Delos, Albion, CA
*The Dance of Selves in Relationship*. Delos, Albion, CA
*Decoding Your Dreams*. Delos, Albion, CA
*Meet the Pusher*. Delos, Albion, CA
*Meet Your Inner Critic*. Delos, Albion, CA
*Meeting Your Selves*. Delos, Albion, CA
*Understanding Your Relationships*. Delos, Albion, CA

## *Videotapes*

Gawain, Shakti: *The Path of Transformation*. Videotape of live talk.
    Hay House, Inc., 1992.

# Workshops

Shakti Gawain gives talks and leads workshops all over the United States and in many other countries. She also conducts retreats, intensives, and training programs. If you would like to be on her mailing list and receive workshop information, contact:

Shakti Gawain, Inc.
P.O. Box 377, Mill Valley, CA 94942
Telephone: (415) 388-7140
Fax: (415) 388-7196
E-mail: staff@shaktigawain.com
Web site: www.shaktigawain.com

For information about Drs. Hal and Sidra Stone's
workshops and trainings, contact:

Delos
P.O. Box 604, Albion, CA 95410
Telephone: (707) 937-2424
E-mail: delos@mcn.org
Web site: www.delos-inc.com

Nataraj Publishing, a division of
New World Library, is dedicated
to publishing books and tapes that inspire
and challenge us to improve the
quality of our lives and our world.

Our books and tapes are available
in bookstores everywhere. For a catalog
of our complete library of fine books
and cassettes contact:

Nataraj Publishing/New World Library
14 Pamaron Way
Novato, CA 94949
Tel: (415) 884-2100
Fax: (415) 884-2199
Or call toll-free: (800) 972-6657
Catalog requests: Ext. 50
Ordering: Ext. 52
E-mail: escort@nwlib.com
Web site: www.newworldlibrary.com